Praise

"With so many introductory books in print, a common question among readers of magical works is 'Where can I go from here?' *Slow Magic* by Anthony Rella wonderfully answers this question. Packed with insight and expertise from Anthony's many years as a witch and therapist, alongside potent exercises and opportunities for reflection and growth, this book is an invaluable addition to the library of any magical practitioner who wants to deepen their practice and create powerful, beneficial change in their life."

—DURGADAS ALLON DURIEL, author of *The Little Work*

"In a world full of instant gratification and fast-food spirituality, *Slow Magic* is a must-have intelligent guide that goes beyond simple spellwork, highlighting the importance of patience, context, and interconnectedness of living magickally. Tony's captivating storytelling and practical wisdom provide a transformative approach to magick, urging readers to embrace their own power and live with purpose. With a wealth of experience in the Feri tradition, Tony strikes a perfect balance between personal insights and universal principles, equipping readers with practical tools for transforming their lives through continual unfoldment of magickal development. What makes *Slow Magic* truly special is its focus on the connections between people, communities, and the environment. This book inspires and empowers you to embrace life's beautiful complexities. It's perfect for anyone wanting to explore the magickal universe on a deeper level and strengthen their sense of connection."

—MAT AURYN, international bestselling author of *Psychic Witch*

"Sometimes what we desire comes from a fanciful whim that does not serve our spirit. While many magical books show us how to perform quick and easy magic, Anthony Rella's *Slow Magic* shows us how to take a moment to express the deeper power within our heart. Rella shows us how mindfulness and being deliberate in our spirituality helps us manifest magic that connects us with the universe and each other for a fulfilling, magical life."

—**CHRIS ALLAUN**, author of *Whispers from the Coven*

"There are two kinds of magic that can be worked in the world. That which is first desired has as its aim a fast resolution to the desired outcome; this is much like flooding a garden after a drought. The plants will drink their fill, and some of them even may thrive. A master gardener may choose to introduce a trickle of water, over a long period of time, to make the entire garden healthier and ensure an abundant yield for a long while. The latter is akin to slow magic. It requires patience, perspective, and vision to take the slower path, but the reader who picks up this book and works through it will come to understand its vast power. Of that, I have no doubt."

—**TERENCE P. WARD**, author of *Empty Cauldrons*

"*Slow Magic* is a stellar and serious work. It is elegant in its simplicity and grounded in its complexity.…Anthony Rella opens us to a profoundly beautiful and workable web of themes, processes, stories, and questions that ennoble the spirit and embolden the heart. *Slow Magic* is a blessing in the form of a book that I hope provokes, invites, and delights readers for years to come, into the deep and rich magic that spirals through time and space."

—**FIO GEDE PARMA**, author of *The Witch Belongs to the World*

"Drawing from modern psychology and ancient spirituality, Slow Magic is a vital antidote to a culture obsessed with quick fixes. Anthony Rella offers creative spells and rituals, solid magical theory, and heart-wise meditations on what it means to journey toward your deepest, fullest self. The witchery in this book is subtle, but it charts a path toward a lifetime of healing."

—**ASA WEST,** author of *Witch Blood Rising* and *The Witch's Kin*

"Magic is the work of a lifetime. So much magical study is focused on what the individual needs in the moment that it can be easy to forget this lifetime work and our relationship with the cosmos over time. *Slow Magic* is like an explorer's guide for a long journey, accompanying your way through the intricate landscapes of your inner self and the phases of your life."

—**DAVID SALISBURY,** author of *The Deep Heart of Witchcraft*

SLOW
MAGIC

About the Author

Anthony Rella (Seattle, WA) is a magic worker and psychotherapist working in private practice. He has been studying and practicing in the Western Esoteric Traditions of witchcraft and magic for more than fifteen years, and he has been a mentor and teacher at the Morningstar Mystery School for the past five years. Anthony is also a founding member and vice president of the Seattle Temple of the Fellowship of the Phoenix. He authored *Circling the Star* and he has contributed nonfiction and poetry to a variety of anthologies. Visit him at AnthonyRella.com.

Slow Magic

Cultivate Lasting Transformation Through Spellwork and Self-Growth

ANTHONY RELLA

Foreword by Ivo Dominguez, Jr.

LLEWELLYN
WOODBURY, MINNESOTA

First Edition
First Printing, 2025

Book design by R. Brasington
Cover design by Kevin R. Brown
Editing by Laura Kurtz
Interior illustrations by Llewellyn Art Department

Llewellyn Publications is a registered trademark of Llewellyn Worldwide Ltd.

Library of Congress Cataloging-in-Publication Data (Pending)
ISBN: 978-0-7387-7708-5

Llewellyn Worldwide Ltd. does not participate in, endorse, or have any authority or responsibility concerning private business transactions between our authors and the public.

All mail addressed to the author is forwarded but the publisher cannot, unless specifically instructed by the author, give out an address or phone number.

Any internet references contained in this work are current at publication time, but the publisher cannot guarantee that a specific location will continue to be maintained. Please refer to the publisher's website for links to authors' websites and other sources.

Llewellyn Publications
A Division of Llewellyn Worldwide Ltd.
2143 Wooddale Drive
Woodbury, MN 55125-2989
www.llewellyn.com

Printed in the United States of America

Acknowledgments

So much love and gratitude to my husband, Jack, for walking this path with me for so long with unflinching acceptance and encouragement. You are truly my partner in life and I am so grateful for you. Thank you to Laura Tempest Zakroff for your important introduction. Thank you to Elysia Gallo for supporting this work and your incisive editorial powers. I am so thankful for my spiritual kin who have shared community with me in Morningstar Mystery School, the Fellowship of the Phoenix, and the Reclaiming tradition. Gratitude also to my teachers and peers in Aikido practice who have shown me the possibilities of community. Gratitude to my teachers of magic, past, present, and future: T. Thorn Coyle, River, Jennifer, Tari, Michael F., Tessa H., Fio Gede Parma, Ivo, Aeptha, Katrina, Dr. Aaron Davis, Zemaemidjehuty, Amanda M., and Matthew E. Gratitude to my teachers of therapy, including every client who has honored me with their trust and vulnerability. Gratitude to my teachers of writing: Brian Bouldrey, Sheila Donohue, John Keene, Evan J. Peterson, and all my peers who challenged me with razor-sharp feedback.

Contents

EXERCISES

FOREWORD

I have been a witch for almost fifty years, so I have felt the effect of magic in the moments, days, months, and years of my life. As soon as I heard the title *Slow Magic*, I felt a strong resonance and a sense of connection with my own experiences of the work. Having now read the book, I find that my intuition has been fully affirmed. I met Tony Rella through my friend T. Thorn Coyle while he was one of Coyle's students. I met him several times over the years at conferences, events, and rituals. Then I found myself reading his writings and connected on social media. My knowledge and appreciation of Tony developed in an unrushed way with no expectations. I came to trust him and his perspectives and as you might guess, I have faith in the worth of his book *Slow Magic*.

This is a book about becoming your magic, transforming yourself, and the shape of the life you inhabit. Guided change of this kind requires more than quick-acting spell work, though that is part of the process as well. Much of this sort of magic relies heavily on the power of context and the reality that is woven from strands of all the beings that make up the world. The book's early chapters invite you to learn from Tony's life experience and his journey into the Feri cosmology. The field of action described is anchored in place by the street-level work of being embodied and the eternal but constantly changing influence of the mythic realm. This slow magic flourishes in between the small and the large in the space that is simultaneously central and liminal.

Although this book is meant for people already working magic, Tony provides ample explanatory material for newcomers. His explanations also help make the book accessible to individuals from a broad range of traditions. After setting the stage, Tony alternates back and forth between introducing and exploring themes and topics and then bringing them to life with rituals and practices. It is not an easy task to shift from self-revelation to illustrating situations and then articulating them as principles that can be used more universally. *Slow Magic* repeatedly finds the middle way without getting muddled.

In an unfortunate number of books that I've read about magical development, there is such a narrow focus on the individual that everything beyond them is a blur. *Slow Magic* shows that we exist in relationship with people, teachers, communities, cultures, and a whole planet of living things. The difficult work that is often the richest and the most life-affirming arises from engaging with all the complexities of the middle world and the middle self. From this cauldron of fates and destinies comes many possible futures, and this book helps to give you the gift of choice and the tools to create the best expression of your life's desires.

Tony Rella's *Slow Magic* is a book that I will be recommending not only to my friends and associates who are magical people, but to any who are open to a broader understanding of the universe. Above and beyond the teachings and the methods shared directly, the whole of this book is encoded with the worldview that life can be joyful, brave, and full of personal myth. I will be reading this more than once, and I hope that you will as well.

Ivo Dominguez, Jr.

Author of *Four Elements of the Wise: Working with
the Magickal Powers of Earth, Air, Water, Fire*

INTRODUCTION

Magic is the art of living joyfully awake and ferociously vital. We are worthy beings who emerge from the earth's innate longings, here to inhabit and express our desire as fully as we can. The practice of spellwork draws upon our spiritual nature to pursue the material fulfillment of desire. Whether we get what we want or not, working magic engages us consciously with the world. We, like all living creatures, feed upon the body of the earth and make it new, make it into our bodies, our descendants, our art. As humans, we create art and technologies to reshape the world according to our instincts and desires. From the perspective of slow magic, however, our manifestations are not things that we do to the world, rather what we create with the multitudinous spirits of the world. Becoming more effective in magic requires befriending and harmonizing the competing urges within us and around us into one alignment that powerfully moves toward what we seek. This teaching instills us with the pride of knowing our birthright for being here and the humility of relationship to the community of beings here with us.

This book is for anyone who practices, or takes interest in, what I think of as the Western magical tradition. This encompasses a variety of approaches that include practitioners who call themselves witches, magicians, Pagans, mystics, alchemists, warlocks, or folk healers. It may include people who identify with a monotheist religion but engage in occult and mystical work. In this work,

I will be examining threads of magical thought and practice found in several different schools and approaches. I have practiced with and learned from Feri, Reclaiming, and Wiccan witches; ceremonial and Chaos magicians; a Hoodoo conjure worker; and a generous Manbo who helped me with a surprising spirit encounter. I have also answered my own personal gnosis calling me to deep relationship with the Kemetic gods. My spiritual home for almost two decades has been with Morningstar Mystery School, an offshoot of the Anderson Feri tradition, and that is the perspective from which I will be speaking in this book.

From my study and practice, I have learned that several spiritual traditions teach that humans have multiple parts of soul with different needs, strengths, and gifts. I was taught this in the form of what is called the triple soul. We will discuss this more, but here is a brief introduction: our animal soul is both animalistic and child-like, playful and feral, deeply embedded in our bodies and a powerful wielder of energy. Our human soul extends further out from the body and tends to be more rational, communicative, giving and receiving information in social connection. Our god soul hovers slightly overhead, containing the unique spark of divinity that chose to incarnate as you, to experience your life, while containing the wisdom and power of countless previous lives and experiences. Bringing these three souls together in cooperation clarifies and empowers our spellwork. When the disparate desires of the souls harmonize into clear intention, we sing out a chord that changes ourselves and the world around us irrevocably. When our parts move together toward a desire, magic is potent, magnetic, alive, full of fear and excitement. We tremble with the power of moving into the unknown. Without this harmony, we flail. Should our animal souls crave what disturbs our human souls, conflict ensnarls magic, causing it to fail or manifest in confusing, unwanted ways.

Following desire leads us to the path of transformation and deep self-knowledge. Knowing with confidence that we can manifest what we need when we need it is wealth greater than money. Greater revelations come when we trace desire into its roots, the desire within the desire, the seed of all desire. As the Star Goddess said: "For behold, I have been with you from the beginning, and I am that which is attained at the end of desire."[1] The source of desire was with us at birth, and in its accomplishment we discover its mystery. Whether the end we attain is disappointment, love, joy, or horror, the whole-hearted pursuit obtains for us the divine within. Magic is the cocoon in which we dissolve and reform into a new being, then discard so that we may pursue desire anew. We start the journey by naming what we know our desire to be today, in this moment. If this seems too esoteric, let me ground this with a story from my life.

Metamorphic Desire

Early in my witchcraft practice, I rarely did spells. Neither did I set goals. I was a "go-with-the-flow, trust-the-Universe" kind of guy. Whenever I remarked upon this, it was with the most relaxed, humble superiority I could muster, like I was so above *wanting things*, unlike everybody else. Yet hidden beneath that armor of detachment was a mess of conflicting longings and fears, anxieties, and feelings of helplessness, envy, jealousy, and competition. In truth, there was a part of me that believed I would never be allowed to have what I desired, so it was better not to want or try. Safer to trust that abstract deity called "the universe" to give what

---

1. Adapted by Starhawk from Doreen Valiente, "The Charge of the Goddess," *The Spiral Dance: A Rebirth of the Ancient Religion of the Great Goddess* (HarperCollins, 1999), 103.

is deemed appropriate. What it gave, though, were bad results. I didn't like myself. I didn't like my body. I didn't know what I had to offer. I squeezed myself into tiny places for others' comfort and concealed my anger behind cynicism. When the time arrived that I was to be thrust out of college and into the working world, I had a crisis. Childhood was not a pleasant time, and I firmly hoped the independence of adulthood would be better territory for me. Yet I had no idea how one forged an adult existence—earning money, finding and keeping jobs, acquiring housing, getting exercise, or cooking regular meals. I was good at school things—writing essays or taking tests. The work of living confused me.

Several of my peers planned to go directly to graduate school, but a wisdom in me knew that route would be postponing, and not solving, this crisis. I needed to face the terror of self-responsibility and commit. When I looked at men in their late twenties and early thirties, I saw a confidence and steadiness that I desired. They were incredibly attractive to me. Knowing this much about what I wanted, I set a long-term goal: to be hot in seven years, when I was the age of those men I admired. Seven years seemed a generous and reasonable expectation, as the conditions of my health and body were not conducive to a more urgent timeline. My friends teased me about my goal. I smoked an average of a half a pack of cigarettes a day and mostly lived on Diet Coke and dorm food. I was shy, lacking direction in life, unathletic, and without an exercise routine. But the distant target gave me a direction, a path, and the patience to take bits at a time. I quit smoking—gradually, with relapses—while beginning to jog. Once I had an exercise routine established, I started to learn what kinds of food nourished my body. I worked on getting a job and a place to live in the city.

At the time, my image of "hotness" came from unhealthy expectations and distorted images of idealized men's bodies. What

I thought my body was supposed to look like was untenable. The diet required for six-pack abs left me unable to sleep through the night out of hunger, causing a rebellion by another part that would voraciously consume beyond the restriction. Over several years of this journey, I learned about the Health at Every Size movement that decouples health from body fat percentage and shows the dangers of dieting. What's more, as I got to know guys with the kinds of builds I envied, I witnessed their continued emotional self-abuse for enjoying an indulgence like the occasional brownie, their continued nitpicking and denigration of their bodies and looks. What's the point of doing all this work and self-denial, I wondered, if you still hated yourself?

In my witchcraft practice during this time, I got to know the goddess Aphrodite. I asked her once, "What makes a person sexy?" She told me it had nothing to do with the shape of one's body. Sexiness is the energy with which you inhabit your body. Her answer helped me to see the charming, lovely, sexy men with bellies who carried themselves with confidence and ease. Getting exercise and eating good food made my body feel good, which helped me to inhabit it with vitality and risk being more sexy in the world. After years, I realized I knew how it felt to be hot without squeezing my body into a shape that didn't fit.

This was my first act of slow magic—setting a long-term intention toward transformation into a sturdy, enduring result. With the attainment of that act came the truth that slow magic also transforms the intention itself. Within the desire of "being hot" was a truer, more profound desire. Staying at the level of "I need to be hot" would mean being vulnerable to losing all that I accomplish whenever a person inevitably did not find me hot. My animal soul craved to feel powerful, sexually connected, and at home in my body. My human soul craved the confidence to be myself wherever I went. My god soul has always and ever wanted me to learn to accept myself fully, love myself, and center in my own energy and aliveness. All my parts came into alignment with this intention, and desire gave my will the fuel it needed to keep going when there were setbacks and losses.

Remembering the work of this desire, twenty years later, I feel gratitude and compassion for that younger me who wanted so much to be loved and felt so wracked with insecurity. Because of that first act of will, that first spell, I feel more deeply in love with my body and its capability, its strength and vitality, its sensuality, and its beauty. Humiliating childhood experiences no longer feel so charged, no longer limit me with their stories. All of those deeper desires continue to manifest and evolve as I age and know myself in new ways. And there are moments when I still feel insecurity, when parts of me still feel small or ashamed, when parts of me feel they don't belong in athletic spaces. There are times when I look at the mirror through the eyes of that more mainstream, fault-finding gaze, but there are more times when I feel love and pride. This journey had been far richer and more interesting than if I had set my original goal as, "I need six-pack abs so I can look good."

Why Slow Magic?

Most of us wish for quick, simple fixes to resolve our problems and let us relax. Why wouldn't we? Life is hard enough. Why is everything so much work? Who has the energy for it? Moving too quickly and expecting too much of ourselves, unfortunately, sets us up to fail. Have you ever—like me—resolved to get your whole life together and committed to a regime of changes all at once? For example: "My new year's resolution is that I'm going to clean my house every week, I'm going to cook breakfast every morning after meditating for a half hour, I'm going to go for a walk after work every night, and I'm going to quit drinking." And maybe for the first week you do a great job executing that plan, and you feel great! You write a long fake-humble-but-self-congratulatory social media post about the positive changes you're making, implying that everyone in your life should follow your example. And then the second week, perhaps a few things happen that throw you off, and you miss your walks at night, but otherwise you got most of your target and still feel pretty good. And then by week four, you're not walking at all because you're back to drinking immediately after work, then you wake up too late and groggy to do much more than eat a granola bar before going to work again. What happened?

You're not a failure who is incapable of change. You attempted too much, too quickly, and perhaps you were not fully clear about your desires and the conditions in which you worked. Such drastic changes are hard to enact at once. We tend to resist change and maintain the conditions of life as they are, though they may be terrible. Sustainable effort is required to change our conditions and find a new homeostasis. If you'd committed to one of those changes and stuck with it for the month, you may have succeeded and then been able to add another. Urgency alone makes action ineffective. We tend to narrow into stress, self-criticism, despair, and deep frustration. We need to braid that energy into a practice of seeking ever-deeper understanding and clarity with the focus of our long-term goals. There are times when we do need speedy results, but we also need slow magic because truly enduring and transformative work requires time, energy, and diligence. Our efforts to change must be sustained alongside the tasks of living. We need to both push ourselves into discomfort and be gentler with ourselves, because success builds confidence. A small achievement motivates us to keep going, whereas failures discourage us, and too many setbacks drain motivation.

Since I was old enough to start reading spiritual and nonfiction books, I've heard over and over again the message of urgency. Our species wobbles on the precipice of great evolution or great self-destruction. We have no time to *not* act. We must integrate these lessons now! Unfortunately this urgency has not turned our collective momentum away from crisis. We are making important changes in the way we relate to the earth and each other, but long-term consequences are already occurring due to global climate change and the pollution of our lands, air, and water. To reverse these would require an ambitious, slow, long-term collective will that I fear we will not achieve. Perceiving the gravity of my concern, that these changes could be irreversible, filled me with bitter cynicism and a sort of annoying, pointless satisfaction in watching my worst case scenarios begin to play out, like a cosmic "I told you so" that didn't accomplish much. Yet I found living with spite a miserable path. Even amid horrors, a life of joy and meaning is still possible. Having survived at least one apocalyptic event, I see now that none of us truly know how it will be to live through what is to come. There is a freedom in that.

Though we can never predict the future with accuracy, we do better when we act as though we have a future. Living as though there is no tomorrow, though a romantic call to action, also deadens us. Motivation and meaning drains away without a future. Having a goal, seeding possibilities, honoring our values brings us to life. Whether we achieve any of those things is less critical—there is no "happily ever after" in a world that constantly turns and cycles through change. The joy of participating in those changes is what magic offers us. Slow magic allows our desire and intention to guide us over days, months, years. With time comes depth of insight and skill. With perseverant, ongoing effort comes resilience and strong support. We confront what is inescapably real about ourselves, our limitations, our powers, and the conditions in which we are living. We create possibilities where none could exist before. There are experiences we cannot have without the commitment of slow magic. We cannot know what it's like to have a relationship of twenty years if we only go on first dates. We cannot run a successful business if we give up after a couple of months. We cannot know what it's like to have a dog that can perform amazing tricks if we don't dedicate the time to training. We cannot harvest the fruits of our own apple tree if we never plant it.

Long-term magic offers profound wisdom and transformation, and a framework to keep us engaged in our lives for the full span. We nurture the ground for our future selves while we are engaged in the tasks of today. We create communities and works with the hope they will benefit future generations. We continue the magical work of our ancestors who left us wisdom, practices, and tools for staying connected to the spiral of unfolding time.

Working with This Book

This book is written for the practitioner who has experience with spell work and divination. Structured practices will help you to apply or deepen those skills, but we will not be going in depth into the basics. What we will cover together is helpful for anyone at any level of skill or experience, and my hope is that this book could be reread over the years and you could come away with inspiration wherever you are in your work. The words of this book float on the surface of the water as foam. Engaging with the experiential work—both what is offered and what comes to you as you read— allows you to know the depths. Yet, there is no expectation that you must finish all your homework before moving to the next chapter. Some practices in this book could be done several times to good effect, and others take months to years to fully explore. Do not force yourself to do it all in one reading. Do engage with the practices that excite or challenge you. If practices do not call to you, that is okay.

I have written with the broadest possible audience in mind, recognizing that it includes folks with different levels of income and access to resources, different abilities and limitations both cognitive and physical, and different cultural backgrounds and levels of training. If, in reading this work, you find examples or practices that are not accessible or welcoming to you but you can think of an adaptation that would make it better, I encourage you to do that instead. What helps me is to try to understand the intention of the practice and then see if I can reframe it to better fit me. There are several exercises that are meditative by nature. I need a quiet, private space where I won't be interrupted to engage in those practices deeply. Your focus could be improved with music or background noise, or being outdoors. You may prefer to work with a trusted friend or partner nearby and available. My hope for you is safety and relaxation so you can go deeply into your work. You are the one best positioned to find what gives you that experience.

First we will discuss the concept of will and its role in Western occultism, looking at **Will as Spiritual Path**. This chapter will introduce God Herself as both macrocosm and microcosm. The paradoxical unity and multiplicity of God Herself exists within our own personal selves, and we will learn to look at our "parts" in our spiritual work of engaging with other-than-human beings and setting magical intentions that bring harmony. In the next chapter, we'll meet the divine twins as figures of duality and polarity that bring us into the synthesis of the peacock. We'll meet the twins as the polarities of **Destiny and Fate** and get to know the lessons of each. Then we will walk as the peacock into our magical work, **Stepping Onto the Path** of magic by looking more closely at the process of creating spells for ourselves, setting our intentions and listening to what we must do.

We will turn back to the divine twins, but we will take a deeper look at their faces in relationship with time. In **Time as Line** we will explore the linear twin of magical time and how we can relate to, and transform, both our past and future to give ourselves more agency. In **Time as Cycle** we will look at the cyclical twin of magical time and study the patterns of recurrence that arise in nature and astrology. All of these will give rise to **Time as Spiral**, which we will explore using the polarity to accept both what is and what is not within our control while moving toward our desire. Then we will return to the divine twins, in their aspects of **Being and Doing**, looking at our magical relationship with effort and ease, assertion and surrender. Then we will take a step back to reflect upon **Traps and Fear** that arise in the magical life, both habits and beliefs that can become hindrances to our continued growth and spiritual development.

The next two chapters, **Working with Spirit** and **Spirit Allies of Slow Magic**, will walk through our relationship to the spiritual world. We will explore a contemplative approach to spiritual work and how this relationship aids our magic in efficacy, and then explore relationships with various families of spirits. **The Compass of Community** will offer a framework for working with other humans on long-term magic. We will then turn toward **Adversities**, particularly the phenomena of resistance and unexpected consequences that arise from deep magical practice. Finally, we will move into **Releasing and Renewing**, exploring processes for reassessing our goals, dreams, and spells, and workings that will help us to renew our work, renegotiate what is no longer workable, or release what no longer serves. This book is crafted as the arc of a spell itself, beginning with the knowing of will, and ending with its release and surrender, so that our will may be refreshed and renewed, ready for its next working.

Chapter 1

WILL AS
SPIRITUAL PATH

Every year, around Samhain, I divine for guidance about the upcoming cycle of the sun. When doing this working in 2022, I shuffled and cut my tarot deck into three piles, as I was taught to do by my teachers. Generally, I sense into which pile feels "right" and select it for pulling the reading. This year, however, I perceived the god I'd called upon for aid pausing me. They reached out and touched each of the piles, giving them names. "This is the path of will. This is the path of desire. This is the path of longing. You must pick your path." The distinctions puzzled me. "Aren't those all the same?" English is a language riddled with the scars of domination, containing both words imposed upon it from dominating forces, and words it plundered from other languages. I wondered whether these various shades of meaning were distinctions without difference.

Consider for yourself: "Will" carries a root of "wish" that still exists in the German use of the word (*Wollen*, "to want"). But English speakers use "will" in a more active sense of moving intentionally toward a goal, with vigor. "Desire" relates to an experience of absence—but not a passive absence. Much is missing from our day-to-day lives that mean nothing to us. I have no elephants at home and no want of one. A desire is an emotionally charged absence, motivating us to seek it and experience its presence. "Longing" has the connotation of lengthening and extension, of reaching for what we cannot grasp. Yet the god responded, "No. They are not the same. You must choose." So I chose the path of will, and upon that path I have written this book. After the reading, I asked for a vision of the three paths to better understand more deeply what had been offered. Each offers a virtue and a trial, and I believe the long work of slow magic will have us walking each over time. Here is a poem that came from my contemplations.

A God Offers the Choice of Three Paths

The Path of Will
Arrow's tip parting air,
committed velocity
forsaking origin
to pierce, utterly change—
even misses leave marks.

The Path of Desire
Hedge of roses, a maze
tempting lost ones to taste
thorns, grasping for blooms,
missing the open path
to satiety's center.

The Path of Longing
A vast and winding road
beneath starlit expanse
upon which empty hands,
aching, lift in wonder,
and nothing reaches back.

Will in the Western Magical Tradition

Will is the common ingredient in several definitions of magic offered by our occult forebears. My own long-time magical teacher, T. Thorn Coyle, defines magic as "the marriage of breath, will, and desire."[2] The focus on will differentiates us from other paths that focus on experiences such as submission or surrender to deity, attempting to perfect the self to transcend this world, or shedding illusions to come into greater understanding of reality. The worker of magic may be a devotee, a healer, a mystic, a warrior, and more—but with these, we must accept and own that we are *an agent*. Will expresses our vital force, our power that wants to emerge through us into this world. What distinguishes an act of will from any other behavior is the presence of consciousness and choice. We are never not interacting with the world, shaping and being shaped by it. Yet when there is no presence, no consciousness, no choice-fulness, we are not engaging will. To illustrate this: notice your breathing. You have been breathing the entire time you have read this passage, and you will breathe after you put down this book and move on to other things. Breathing is an automatic act, but it also has the potential of being an act of will. Decide now to take in a deep breath, hold it for a moment, and then exhale completely—that is an act of will. Your conscious awareness steps forward to direct your action. You are *there* while it happens.

Will influences the world through the expression of our powers. We act on purpose and influence what must happen. We speak up about a concern. We answer or ignore a demanding message. We protest on the street. We submit paperwork to start an organization. We carve a piece of wood with the blade of a knife, making

---

2. T. Thorn Coyle, *Kissing the Limitless: Deep Magic and the Great Work of Transforming Yourself and the World* (Weiser, 2009), viii.

art from nature. Slow magic begins with this notion of will and agency as that faculty within us that is able to show up and participate. Some paths exalt the personal will over all other relationships and considerations, while other paths surrender the personal will to one that is larger and more mysterious. With slow magic, we walk with one foot on each path, shifting our weight left then right, treading the mystery between. To will is to be in engaged relationship. Not to receive or be buffeted about, not to demand or command. Rather, to contribute our ideas, energy, skills, and desires; and to be met by those of another.

EXERCISE
Basics of Will Development

Cultivating will is as simple and challenging as setting an intention to act and following through. Try doing this for a week, every day. For this practice, it's useful to change a habit that is not emotionally charged. Don't try for any huge goals that would bring up intense feelings. Instead pick a simple, automatic habit that would require effort to change and commit to doing so for a week. A couple ideas to consider: If you carry your phone in your pocket always on one side, try switching to the other for a week. Alternately, you could resolve to be outside for five minutes a day, every day. Another possibility: get out of bed ten minutes earlier than you usually would. These are simply suggestions to encourage you to come up with an idea that is achievable but slightly challenging.[3]

---

3. For more suggestions on tasks you can do to develop will, I like the list offered by Durgadas Allon Duriel in *The Little Work: Magic to Transform Your Everyday Life* (Llewellyn Publications, 2020), 197–200.

Should you forget your intention or default to the usual habit, acknowledge that it happened and adjust your behavior. If you miss a whole day, recommit to the action and follow through as soon as possible. Acknowledge any self-judgment or self-criticism, but do not allow it to convince you that you must now give up altogether or restart the clock. What's more important is that you return to the original commitment. If you struggle, journal about which parts of you might be having a hard time with this effort. As you do this exercise, you may notice that other effortful habits slip, a temporary and normal result of this effort to strengthen your will. It's like starting a new and intense form of physical exercise. Afterward, your muscles feel weaker for a while. But with rest, repair, and consistency, there will be an overall improvement in strength.

Executive Functioning

Will relates to what is called executive functioning in psychology, the capacity of the brain to remember relevant details, consider multiple perspectives, think about the consequences of actions, and inhibit impulsive behavior so we can engage in intentional actions. From what we know today, the part of our brain responsible for these functions is known as the prefrontal cortex, a relatively recent evolutionary addition to the nervous system that shows up in rodents and primate groups with a particular expansion of function in humans.[4] The prefrontal cortex begins to develop in adolescence but does not reach full maturity until around the age of twenty-four.

---

4. Todd Preuss and Steven Wise, "Evolution of prefrontal cortex," *Neuropsychopharmacology* 47 (2022): 3–19.

The basic hardware of our nervous system—the spinal cord—evolved with our vertebrate animal cousins and governs a robust set of functions to help animals survive long enough to reproduce. This was so successful that, instead of developing a whole new nervous system, evolutionary mutations expanded the functions of the spinal cord and added additional hardware on top of it. The cerebellum enhances our muscle control and balance. The limbic system organizes emotion, behavior, and memory, helping us to learn from experience so we can care for our young and use our fight and flight responses. The prefrontal cortex is the most recent hardware installation for an operating system that has existed in rudimentary forms for millennia. It has the capacity to suppress our limbic responses when we are well-rested, fed, relaxed, and well-resourced to make use of its functions.

Say you were walking down the street, and someone jumped out at you and yelled "Boo!" Your limbic system might want to launch the fight response, sending blood to your arms and legs and flooding you with adrenaline so that you can kill this threat before it has a chance to harm you or your loved ones. But your prefrontal cortex, knowing that killing another person invites unwanted long-term consequences such as guilt and prison time, pauses the fight response long enough for you to assess that it's your best friend trying to scare you and not a threat that you need to eradicate. Since it is the most recent addition, however, it's also the first to decrease in efficacy when we're under stress.[5] While enduring a life-threatening situation, our bodies are more likely to turn off nonessential functions—such as thinking about consequences and reflecting on our behavior—and focus all resources on the fight, flight, or freeze threat responses. With our executive functioning impeded, we're more

---

5. Amy F. T. Arnsten, "Stress signalling pathways that impair prefrontal cortex structure and function," *Nature Reviews, Neuroscience* 10, no. 6 (2009): 410–22.

likely to punch first—or run away or collapse—before assessing the situation thoroughly.

What our nervous systems consider "life-threatening" begins with signs of unmet basic needs—hunger, thirst, fatigue—and extends toward the more symbolic threats we've learned through culture and life experience. Our threat response systems become more sensitized in response to danger and major, ongoing stress. Unsettling and violent traumas such as war, imprisonment, and natural disasters add more stress and ongoing concern for safety. A childhood of chaotic living environments, violence, or neglectful caregivers sets us up for a life of constant vigilance. Other pervasive stressors include ongoing threats of physical, social, or economic violence due to our skin color, ancestry, class, or how well we fit into the dominant culture. Along with stress and trauma, other conditions impair our executive functioning, such as attention deficit hyperactivity disorder, forms of autism, poverty, and living in a culture with constant conflicting demands upon our time and technological bids for our attention.

All of us have the capacity to strengthen will with practice. All of us struggle when we attempt to strengthen our will. Some of us struggle more or in different ways than others, and that's not a sign of badness or incapacity. Be gentle with yourself, and consider the whole context: How is your sleep? Are you drinking enough water? Are you eating enough? Are you overwhelmed by stressors? Is constant multitasking draining your brain? Do you live on constant alert because you've been hurt and the world is an unsafe place? Might you have a neurological condition that makes executive functioning harder? Addressing these questions is beyond the scope of this work, but if you struggle with will-building and do not have a clear understanding of why, consider these questions as avenues to explore. Your will work could be starting there: Drinking water more frequently. Examining your sleep habits. Creating safety in your life. If you have the resources, you might pursue a psychological assessment or see a therapist. If you don't have the resources for professional support, there are an array of online communities of people who struggle with attention and focus who offer a wealth of hard-earned wisdom you could explore. Continuing to read this book, and engaging with the exercises you can, is also an act of will.

One practice that improves executive functioning involves learning to soothe the stress response through slowing the breath and relaxing the muscles. When our bodies tense up from stress, our breath naturally becomes more shallow and higher up in the chest, signaling to our nervous system to be alert to threats. The response becomes cyclical—the stress response increases stress, and as that threat response increases, executive functioning decreases. Soothing the threat response, then, increases our available capacity for willful action. Unbinding those stress-inducing mental habits and unprocessed emotional wounds helps stress, but for this practice we will focus on calming the body directly. Through slowing and relaxing, we signal to our nervous systems that we're safe, thereby freeing up our focus for magical work. Approaching stressful situations with calm, relaxed bodies is integral to numerous disciplines, including any kind of martial arts practice. Soft, relaxed muscles are less prone to injury, and a calm mind creates more possibilities than one whose perspective is narrowed by fear and anger. When I lead people through this exercise, I invite them to start by ranking their tension on a scale of 1 (no tension) to 10 (complete tension), and then to rank again at the end.

EXERCISE
Progressive Muscle Relaxation

Sit or lie down, and go through your muscle groups in the following listed order. With each number, breathe in while squeezing and tensing the named muscles as tightly as you can without causing yourself injury or cramping. Hold the breath and squeezing for a few moments, then exhale and let go of the tension. I do each muscle group twice before moving to the next.

Start with squeezing the toes, curling them in and engaging the soles of both feet.

Lift the toes, engaging and clenching the ankles and calves.

Squeeze the hamstrings, quadriceps, and buttock muscles.

Engage the pelvic floor, squeezing the anus and the muscles you would use to stop yourself from urinating.

Tighten the abs.

Clench the pecs, bringing your arms slightly forward.

Clench the back, puffing your chest forward and squeezing your shoulder blades together.

Make both fists tight.

Tilt your fists to engage the forearms, lifting the elbows to engage the biceps. Let both arms drop as you exhale.

Lift your shoulders toward your ears and squeeze the neck.

Engage the jaw, imagining that you're biting down on a rope or a piece of leather. Try not to grind your teeth together but engage your jaw with the bite.

Squeeze all the muscles of your face and head.

Check in and notice if there are any places of tension
    left. Engage those muscle groups with another breath
    or two. Finish by breathing in and clenching all the
    muscles in your body, holding for a long beat, and
    then exhaling, letting yourself relax and soften.

You could be more thorough depending on how deeply
you want to relax. For example, you could flex one toe at
a time or one leg at a time, moving slowly up your body.
Often, people new to this work will start to yawn and feel
tired, which is usually a sign that the system has shifted
out of threat mode and into "rest and digest" mode. Occasionally you may feel more energized or buzzing. If it's too
much, press your feet into the ground and imagine the earth
helping you hold the excess energy. Occasionally when we
do progressive muscle relaxation, the increased awareness of
our bodies makes us more conscious of how much tension
we're holding. You've done a lot of work to repair the connection between mind and body, animal and human souls.

Willing in Relationship

The cultural legacy of the Victorian age blends will with an ethos
of imperialistic dominance and forcefulness. Instead of holding
our will as one node webbed to thousands of other wills, we bear a
cultural burden in the belief that will is essentially a solitary activity by a lone deified individual acting upon the world according
to their precise aims. Relational will connects us to process rather
than fixates on outcome. It is as much contemplation as action.
We set goals to orient us in a direction—wanting to win an award,

learn a skill, or feel more at peace in life—but the journey works us as much as we work it, and the destination remains a mystery.

Will makes us present, alive, and involved in the process of moving toward the goal. My goal in writing this book included a hope for it to be published and a dream of it being well received, feeding the work of others. All my will governed was my ability to sit and write until the book was done, to hone and sharpen the craft, and submit the work for others to consider. Beyond the limits of my power is how others receive and respond to it and what life it will live in the world. To fixate on a specific outcome makes us tense and inflexible, prone to injury. If my will requires that I must experience success with no criticism, mistakes, missteps, or failure, then I've set myself up for an incredibly rough and discouraging journey. Magical practice is beautiful in that it invites mystery and adventure into our lives, where setbacks or derailments become the most memorable and important moments of the journey.

Two major misapprehensions about will that we will continue to explore through this work lie in the extremes of "I control everything" and "I control nothing." Neither position works, and both drain us of our vitality and motivation. If you feel you are or must be in control of everything, then you never get a break. You must monitor and observe yourself and your surroundings at all times. You experience setbacks and mistakes as personal failures and signals of your worst fears. You mistrust others and yet feel responsible for them. You are likely more tense and irritable than you'd like to be. If you feel you are in control of nothing, then you are buffeted about by circumstance and defeated by all setbacks and conflicts. You struggle to summon the motivation to try, and hope is the most dangerous feeling of all because it invites more painful disappointment. You may defer to others and expect them to make all the choices and do all the work.

Both stories center the "I" and distort our relationships. Work on the self shows us how little we control even our own thoughts, feelings, and behaviors—let alone those of others—and also the external circumstances that affect our plans. We struggle to act because conflicting thoughts, feelings, and behaviors each point to different values that need harmony. With practice, we find how we can exert will in our bodies and begin taking risks. We learn to pause our bodies before they shout hurtful words. We take ourselves for a walk instead of sitting frozen in the anxiety-ridden story of our powerlessness. We complete and submit the job application even as loud parts of us accuse us of being worthless and stuck. Befriending our thoughts, feelings, and behaviors aligns them into a will that's true and durable. When you know what you want, it is like standing on one side of an enormous river and seeing your desire on the other shore. Seeing this, parts of us may want to sit and bemoan our fate. Parts of us may want to try to swim across, stubbornly fighting the current until we exhaust ourselves or end up several miles downstream from where we wanted to go. Parts of us may want to give up and be at peace with what's already on our side of the river. Crossing the river is the act of will. Casting a spell builds a boat that can carry you across the water. Prayer and divination show you where to launch your boat so you can work wisely with the river's currents to get to where you want to be.

Here's a time in my own life when I needed to accept which way the river flowed: During a major recession after moving across the country, I was in trouble. The kinds of jobs I'd been working at weren't available. I'd worked as a content editor for about $20 an hour at my last job, but now there were few positions available to the glut of laid-off and better-qualified people hunting them. Being in a new city, relying wholly upon my partner's income, I froze with the intense anxiety that if I couldn't get that kind of job at that income, I'd be totally lost. It was that inner sense of shame and unworthiness that told me no one would stay with me through difficult times; there would be no one to catch me. I was doing many, many spells around getting the kind of job I used to have, but nothing took. I had to step back and take an honest look. First of all, I needed to accept that the recession was happening and stop taking it personally. It wasn't my fault, it wasn't being done to me, and I couldn't swim against that current. Next, I needed to accept that I hated content editing and corporate work and had already been dreaming of changing careers. Fighting both realities in the effort to get back to where I had been made my magic panicky, weak, and unskillful. Next, I recognized I needed income, as I didn't qualify for unemployment in this new state. So I found minimum wage work—at the time, about $7.75 per hour—first at a gas station, then a coffee shop, which gave me a moment to ground. Then I explored going back to school to become a therapist. Working as a barista for the next four years gave me the flexibility to do school without going into debt as severely.

Sailing with this new current took me into a career that suited me much better and protected me when further shocks and crises came down the line. Though this was a trying time, I feel so much gratitude that I *couldn't* find another corporate job I would hate. Slow magic slows us down so we can look more deeply into the drives that push us toward magic. Not to see what's on the other side of the river and feel we want it, but to sink more deeply into what it means to us, whether parts of us don't want it, and better assess what magic needs to occur for our wills to be strongly wound together.

Shame and Moralism

Acts of will are neither good nor bad. Willful acts can cause great harm, and they can redeem. Neither is inherent goodness or worthiness essential to whether we achieve the results of our will. Workers of magic get in their own way when they worry about whether they deserve their will, or try to reassure themselves with, "I'm a good person, of course I deserve it!" Persistence, perseverance, luck, and our ability to influence circumstances allow us to achieve what we will. Those unencumbered by guilt, shame, or questions of worthiness have an easier time pursuing their goals than those who worry about whether they are deserving. Shame, guilt, and the moralizing attitude are impediments placed by the human soul against the animal soul's powers of will. Our human soul is what concerns itself with social relationships, conditioned by the expectations of our families and cultures as to what behaviors are acceptable. Guilt tells us when we are out of alignment with our own values, and it may be burdened with distortions. We may have learned from an early age to put others before our own needs and thus feel guilt for caring for ourselves in ways that are completely mature and responsible.

When we feel a deep sense of shame, unworthiness, or lack of merit, we have likely experienced a threat of being cast out from a group. In a sense, shame keeps us bound in respect for communal norms—we know certain behaviors are beyond acceptability and will cause us to get exiled. As with guilt, however, our young experiences with bullying, social norms, or learning the boundaries of relationships may burden us with inordinate feelings of shame about thoughts and feelings that are not so terrible when said out loud. Or we grew up without a sense of rootedness and belonging, believing that all love is conditional based on what we can do for others and not given to us because we are innately worthy. We may grow skilled in making ourselves indispensable to others to win their love and dependence, and we may learn to keep pushing away love and connection. Both response have at their heart the terror of losing connection, which gives others a great deal of our power.

Expressing will, at its foundation, asserts that I belong here and what I desire is worthy. Fear, shame, and guilt threaten to smother the fire, but if we stoke its flames, the heat and vitality of will offers healing and relief to those terrified parts of us. We grow confident in being who we are, knowing we can create belonging wherever we need it. Whether you moralize about your own or others' motivations is your business, but I find it generally not very useful. No matter what we "should" or "shouldn't" want or believe, most of us carry desires, thoughts, and feelings that contradict the ways we want others to see us. Refusing to acknowledge them does not make them go away, but turns them into monsters that become more disturbing and demanding of our respect and recognition.

Will Is a Twisted Rope of Many Strands

Myriad microorganisms live within your body, cells, and organs that both help and hinder you in your life. You are whole, and you are manifold. You may go through life knowing little about this multiplicity, or life may compel you to become intimately familiar with the processes of your muscles, your heart, your gut biome, your nervous system. So when we imagine that will is complete control of one's self and one's reality, the question arises—*whose* control? Are we driven by our animal soul's instincts, needs, and wants? Are we ruled by the human soul's rationality or fears of the actions of others? Are we inspired by the god within us, potent yet disinterested in mundane matters such as money, bills, or debt?

Authenticity emerges when every part of us is included. There is not one part of us more valid than the others.

This book is informed magically by Morningstar Mystery School and psychologically by Internal Family Systems Therapy. As mentioned in the introduction, I've learned from my studies that there is a multiplicity of "parts of self" that compete or collaborate with each other. We are a singular being with a multiplicity of consciousnesses within us. The loving and infinitely patient presence of our god soul helps to bring those parts into harmony with each other. There are almost immeasurable parts. You can work with your rational and animal souls as parts. You can work with a four-fold elemental structure of body, mind, heart, and will as parts. Some parts must be met on their own terms, unmapped by any system of personality.

All of our parts want our greatest good but perceive the world in a narrow, rigid way. These limitations narrow the range of possibilities for being, which quickly becomes unbalanced, so we develop other parts to compensate for the limits of one. As an example, some of us are deeply identified with driven, ambitious parts that want to devote every waking moment to working—which is untenable. We don't know how to turn off. So another part comes along to force us to take a break by doing things like getting drunk or high, scrolling through the internet, or feeling ill and being forced to relax. This very clever balancing leads to a lot of internal fighting—we think one part must be good and the other bad. Spiritual practice and inner work offer the cultivation of conscious presence to end the battle. When we are there but do not take sides, we learn to honor each part's wisdom, find what is valid within their perspectives, and use this information to make the best choice for the whole. We twist these strands of hope, fear, and desire into one strong rope, which is the truest will.

Within us is an innate goodness and drive toward connection and harmony. Yet the real danger and uncertainties of living in this world compel us to form protective systems that keep us safe but divided from that quality of our being. Without compassionate and firm presence, our parts go to extremes and cause real harm. When we see this harm, we may start to fear that compassion toward a destructive impulse is indulgence that allows it to run wild. In my experience, the opposite is true. Approaching ourselves with judgment and confrontation invites resistance and conflict. Compassion and understanding soften that resistance and make us open to real change. Exploring the roots of these destructive patterns reveals how it has been necessary for our own safety and well-being. Acknowledging this good intention does not mean giving permission to the harmful behavior. Instead, the understanding lets the part come out of the shadows and sit with the rest of us, including our ethics and divine nature.

In this multiplicity, we are a fractal iteration of the larger being of whom we are a part called God Herself. Victor Anderson spoke of God Herself as the stellar goddess in whom we live, move, and have our being, countering the dominant patriarchy by foregrounding femininity. Sometimes I refer to "God Hirself" instead, with pronouns such as "hir" and "they" to foreground the queer aspects of this totality. This god encompasses all beings and thus is of no gender and all genders. We express her being through our unique experience. We are an atom in the enormous body of God Herself, distinct but part of the whole. All of us, even the people we hate. Even the rocks, the ferns, the butterflies, and the tardigrades. Each of us is here to experience what it is to be exactly what we are. Within this totality are countless currents of will, multitudes of beings with agency in this and other worlds. All these may align into one larger current of will, which would be so vast and incomprehensible to us that it does not seem useful to contemplate. Yet without a center of presence able to hold, witness, and love these currents, they act according to their own energies. They may be chaotic and at odds within us and in the totality. Turning toward our inner worlds with presence, care, and the divinity of God Herself creates space for what is within to begin to flourish in love. Turning toward the gods in prayer and attention, particularly God Herself, helps us to flourish in accord with what is without.

Working with a Part: Basics

Let us look more deeply at inner conflicts around will and desire between parts of self. We will start with personal psychology, drawing upon the Internal Family Systems approach, but these skills are applicable throughout this book.[6] They are simple, which makes them tricky to practice. Notice your responses to the material presented here. If you feel angry, suspicious, bored, dismissive—if you think it's garbage—or if you feel confused, eager, doubtful, or earnestly believing—note any experience you have. Notice the thoughts in your mind. Notice what's happening in your body on the level of physical sensations. Notice if a part of you is trying to make sense of the sensations, and see if you can relax that and instead describe what you sense is happening. Do you feel tense, tired, energized? Heavy? Warm? Cold?—descriptors like that. Take three deep breaths, exhaling completely and letting yourself pause a moment before you inhale again. Imagine that these thoughts

---

6. If you are curious about exploring Internal Family Systems further as a therapy practice, I recommend Richard C. Schwartz's *No Bad Parts* (Sounds True, 2021). The IFS Institute maintains a listing of practitioners at https://ifs-institute.com/.

and feelings are their own being inhabiting your body. This being is you—it's a part of you. There's no need to make it go away or change what it's doing. You're wanting to get to know it as if it's a friend who has been with you for years and suddenly you're like, "Hey, I don't know much about you." Imagine this part could sit beside you in the room you're in, or that it could take a denser form in your body with which your consciousness could converse.

EXERCISE
Asking and Listening

Ask this part of you, described on the previous page, to tell you how it serves you. Wait, and observe what happens in your body and mind as a response. You may get words, you may get memories, you may get sensations, or a kind of knowing. If you notice yourself trying to analyze, figure out, or predict the response, consider that a part of yourself trying to understand this other part. Turn toward this analyzer or figure-outer instead, and ask it how it serves you. Next, whenever you notice yourself having any kind of reaction, especially if it feels emotionally "big," try to check in with it in this way. Check in with parts that have big emotional reactions as well as parts that do not like those parts. Ask what it wants you to know. If it's overwhelming, ask it to distill its message to its greatest concern. See what it needs from you.

Not "Just a Part"

You may hear the word "parts" with an implicit bias: "Oh, that's a part of you, that's not who you are." That is not the attitude I want to convey. Our parts are who we are—all of them. They hold all of our memories, our drives, our motivations, our needs and wants.

The problem arises when we pick sides and think one or two of them are "good" or "authentic" and dismiss the others. That judgment leads to fighting and power struggles. Authenticity emerges from being fully present with all of our parts. Our god soul has come to be embodied in us to experience the full range of who we are. Being present and aligned with god soul, its font of witnessing, love, and acceptance, allows our parts to develop and flourish into their fullest expressions, in harmony with our other parts.

As god soul is to our parts, so God Herself is to all of us. We live in a world of vast multiplicity and difference with interconnection. As Pagans and magic workers, we may have a deep relationship to gods and spirits who embody discrete truths and realities about existence. Our martial gods may feel in tension with those gods of love, beauty, and harmony. As people, we find we are drawn to some folks and repulsed by others, and there are still others with whom we cannot fathom any kind of relationship. Yet with all this difference is a totality in which we all exist, and affect and are affected by each other. That totality is God Herself.

God Herself is no cruel judge, no taskmaster, no militant ruler who looks at us and finds us disappointing, deficient, or bad unless we adopt their stringent discipline. God Herself admires us for being reflections of who they are, and in our infinitely diverse expressions, God Herself can experience their totality and multiplicity. In connecting with God Herself, we can be fully who we are, our fullest expression of being, and sense the harmonizing chords within the discord of life. Connecting to this being, this totality, helps us see the relationships and interconnections between things and find our place within that totality. It is like how the gravity of the sun allows for the disparate planets, moons, and asteroids of our solar system to sustain harmonious orbits. This harmony improves our magic. When we allow all of ourselves to participate in intention-setting, we create magic that works for who and where we are today. When we refuse parts a place at the table, then we have to worry about "self-sabotage," because sabotage is the last refuge of the dispossessed. If we include their needs and concerns in making the choice, then what would there be to sabotage? Let's try a practice to help with creating this kind of integrated intention.

EXERCISE
Calling the Council

Consider a change you'd like to make in your life, or a spell you want to execute. Find a place where you can feel safe and be uninterrupted for twenty or so minutes. If you have a partner supporting you in this work, they can hold the space and guide you through the exercise, which could help you go deeper into it. Slow down your breathing and feel your connection to the earth. As you exhale, let the earth take more of your weight and take in its support. Do this for several cycles of breath as your body relaxes more. With your eyes opened or closed, imagine a meeting space. A place where you can gather with several people, where you can be in charge of the meeting. It could be a large round table, or an amphitheater, or a stone circle on grass.

Send a call to all of your parts to join you in this circle. You may sense specific parts showing up, or you may sense an enormous multitude. Trust that everyone who needs to be there will be. Tell this council of your parts about the work you want to do, and ask for desires, concerns, or feedback. Do not argue with, dismiss, or immediately adopt what your parts bring, and instruct them not to engage with each other. Let each part get your attention, and speak its piece, and make sure its perspective is heard and understood before moving to the next. If a perspective seems confusing or extreme, ask the part to go deeper in helping you understand. I like the question, "What is important about this to you?" Keep going until you find a deeper concern or desire that makes sense. Parts will have conflicting perspectives, but this phase is about hearing and understanding all perspectives before trying to solve the problem. If too many parts overwhelm you, ask your council to focus on sending one or two of the most influential speakers. Once you feel done, or all the parts that want to participate have shared, consider inviting your spiritual allies to similarly share—any deities, spirits, or other beings that might have a concern or perspective to add.

Now, contemplate an intention that honors all of these needs, desires, and concerns in a harmonious way. If you can come up with an intention, check it out with your council, and keep modifying it until it feels right to you and your parts. If you do not have words, ask for a symbol of this desire. Then ask your council to help you know what it will feel like to fully realize this intention. Let them help you sense in your body that accomplishment. Let that feeling move through you and make any adjustments needed in posture to open up and embody that energy. Thank yourself and your council and let go of this image, coming back to your body. Feel the ground below you. Drink water. Document your intention and the feeling of embodiment, whether by journaling it or making an audio memo of it so you can hold it in your awareness. You can do the work you like with this intention, or you can use it as the basis for working through the upcoming chapters.

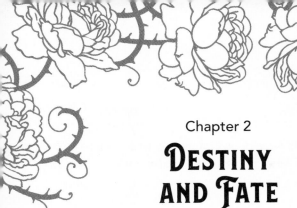

Chapter 2

DESTINY AND FATE

Traversing the currents of slow magic brings us into confrontation with the bigger questions about will, meaning, and control. When enacting big, ambitious magic, we'll have moments of questioning and doubt when it's unclear whether any movement is happening at all or who is piloting the craft. Is it we who draw toward us the moments of beauty and inspiration, the enlivening connections, the joy of accomplishment? Or are we drawn to them, moved like a puppet toward a purpose we never understand or predict? Do our choices matter? Do we welcome or resist the unexpected changes of plan that come with living?

I make an effort to record my dreams, and when I look back, at times I can see that my dreams foretold certain problems. But only in a way that made sense in retrospect. When I worked as a barista, I got to be a lead for a time but then was demoted due to drawing the ire of my manager's manager. The catalyst was a day I was in the back room taking my legally protected lunch break while the others were out front fielding a customer complaint about our lack of silverware, a problem created by my manager's underestimation of how much we would need to order. They could have run to get silverware from a connected restaurant, but they didn't. According to my manager, I wouldn't have been considered responsible if I'd left the building entirely for my half hour of lunch, but I didn't. My manager's manager thought that my heart was no longer in the job, as I was finishing up graduate school and preparing to leave for my next career, and so it was convenient to honor the complaint by demoting me. As a long-time people pleaser, I felt humiliated.

Later, flipping through an old dream journal, I happened upon an entry dated months prior to the incident where I dreamt my manager's manager was interfering with my career. Thanks for the warning, dream self! What good had it done? If I'd taken it seriously, I might have ingratiated myself upon my manager's manager to avoid the problem. Yet there was truth in her concern—my heart was flagging. I was working six or seven days a week between school and my job. I resented the customer service life and could not wait to start a career where I might be treated with respect instead of as disposable labor. The dream perhaps showed an inevitable hand pushing me out of the comfort of the familiar onto my path. What meaning I choose reflects my sense of the relationship between destiny and fate. We will explore those big perspectives in this chapter, calling upon the divine twins as mentors in this work.

Meeting the Divine Twins

From the totality of God Herself emerges the divine twins, beings of opposition and complementarity, love and conflict. They embody all dualities, all polarities. Her rage dances with his sorrow. His darkness sharpens her brightness. Her reason clarifies his depth. When I call to the twins, I perceive a figure of brightness and a figure of darkness. What qualities I associate with each tends to change from day to day, and this mutability is one of their mysteries. To say, for example, that the masculine is bright and the feminine is dark is one truth, and it is also true that the bright one is feminine and the dark one is masculine, and it is true that both twins could be the same gender, or no gender at all.

Working with the divine twins brings forward a needed perspective on paradox, conflict, and balance. One cannot exist without the other, and both are necessary. We may prefer one to the other, but we cannot escape either. Though this duality is misleading—an expression of our limits in perceiving totality—the twins clarify what would be an undifferentiated mess of experience. They embody both the strengths and limitations of each end of a polarity while subtly revealing the underlying unity between them. They are two seemingly opposing approaches to a common problem, two perspectives of a common reality. Throughout this book, the twins will show up to help us find paradox and the middle path of slow magic. The dark twin will ground us in the mysteries of fate, cyclicity, and being, while the bright twin will reveal the mysteries of destiny, linearity, and doing. I urge you not to fall into the habit of thinking one twin is "good" and the other "evil." More useful is to look at the good and evil natures of each twin, twins within twins. With this multiplication, the mystery of God Herself and the twins expresses a mystery akin to what is written in the *Tao Te Ching*: "The Way bears one. / The one bears two. / The two bear three. / The three bear the ten thousand things."[7]

EXERCISE
Meeting God Herself and the Divine Twins

Get two candles of the same length and substance. One should be white and the other black, but I also use two white candles and set them in contrasting clear and dark

---

7. Lao Tzu, "Children of the Way," *Tao Te Ching*, trans. Ursula K. Le Guin (Shambhala, 1997), 52.

candle holders. You will also want a black candle to represent God Herself.

Place the God Herself candle on a surface and the two twin candles on either side of it. Light the candle of God Herself and imagine the vastness of empty space. Feel how it is to be in a world with no separation, no differentiation, where all is blended and blurred, chaotic and whole. As you light the white candle for the bright twin, imagine a shaft of light piercing this world, creating contrast and separation. With this light, God can see Herself reflected in the bowl of space. Light the black candle for the dark twin, imagining both the illumination and the dark reflection of God Herself falling in love and joining together in passion.

Keep breathing, and notice that God Herself is the container for this experience. As the twins make love or fight, notice how they define each other, how they blur, whether they seem solid or mutable. Notice the space around them and between them, which is God Herself, as the twins too are God Herself while also distilling a duality within them. Feel in your body how it is to hold this multiplicity of awareness. There is the consciousness that can witness your entire experience, witness your body, witness the twins making love within your soul. And there is the you who is embodied in each of the twins. Let your awareness move into the bright twin and feel how it is to be limited within the totality, to confront your other. Let your awareness move into the dark twin and feel how it is to be what was once other, looking from the outside at what was once familiar.

Stay with this as long as you like, and then thank the twins and God Herself. Extinguish the candles. As we meet the different faces of the twins throughout this book, you might want to return to this exercise and work with those specific facets of duality.

Introducing Destiny and Fate

In this chapter, the divine twins reveal to us the duality of destiny and fate. Though these words are used interchangeably, differentiating them allows for nuance in our relationship to agency, causality, and meaning. Destiny and fate are contrasting responses to the questions of "Who is in charge of my life?" and "Does it matter what I do?" Each answer establishes a clear path to follow while closing off others, particularly when taken to their extremes.

Our destiny is the product of our actions and choices, wholly contingent upon ourselves. We establish the future through the intentions and efforts of the present. Though we have the freedom to change and make new choices, destiny foreshadows the inevitable conclusion of what we choose. If you leave the vegetables unattended in your stove without setting a timer, your destiny may be to cook inedible charcoal. When I first learned to read tarot, I was taught to view the "outcome" cards in this way: this is where your path will lead should you continue to follow it, but you can change course. We have the freedom to choose but not to escape the consequences of our choices.

Fate, on the other hand, denies agency to our choices or actions. What we do and what will become of us is already declared and will come to pass. Perhaps a greater god's will establishes the course of our lives. We observe the actions of fate in the historical circumstances in which we live. No matter how skillful you are at networking or writing a job application, you may be unable to get a certain job because of the influence of a major economic downturn or a bias that has nothing to do with you as a person. Forces beyond us govern what options are available—economic boom or decline, changing climates, technologies that disrupt and permanently change old industries and ways of being. In a sense, fate removes our responsibility for what happens in life. We might have a measure of agency in how we turn toward those governors of fate and petition for their aid. One of those gods might grow fond of you and shelter you from the storm. But at its most distilled, fate is like being held in a tangle of rope that grows tighter and more painful when we struggle against it. The best course of action is to relax and soften.

These distillations illustrate the energies each twin brings by showing them at their most extreme and differentiated. In truth, the twins need not be adversaries demanding we choose a side and reject the other. Instead, they are guardians and teachers. Consider the following story: A young man grew up in a quiet small town, miles away from the nearest railroad. Not many left this town. But as a boy, he found a book about Scandinavia, an exotic place across the ocean. In this book was an effervescent depiction of the great northern lights, the aurora borealis. His heart burned with the longing to tour those lands and, ultimately, to know those lights with the same intimacy and clarity with which he knew the bed he slept in every night.

As he grew into maturity, he prayed for the chance to go up north in his own lands, but no opportunity came—no surprise trips with family, no unexpected contest winnings, no work that could lead him north. There was a fortune-teller passing near his town with the circus, so the young man took the money he had to hear his future.

The fortune-teller laid down three cards and closed her eyes. "Your fate is to grow old in the place where you were born."

"What about the northern lights?" the young man wondered.

"Fate has nothing to say about the lights."

Despondent, the young man fell into a depression for a few years. He withdrew from his old friends and spent little time with family, instead working enough to afford his one-room home. One day, his mother surprised him with a visit. She confronted him about his attitude and how rarely he came to see her these days. Crying, the young man confessed the whole story—his longing, the refusal of fate to honor his wish.

His mother scoffed. "This is a ridiculous thing to cry about. If you want to see the lights, go see the lights. I'll give you the money if it means you stop moping."

Now the young man was filled with excitement and vigor, but in all his agony he'd never thought through what would be necessary to make the journey. He spent several months looking at travel routes, researching the best places to see the lights and when, as well as what he would need to go. During that time, his mother began to fall ill. Her body grew sallow and slack, and she forgot what she was doing in the midst of her daily life. The family worried about her, but she was firm about staying in her own house. The young man was the only one unmarried and unattached, and it seemed natural the responsibility would fall to him to go live with his mother and help her through her illness.

He grew despondent again. He raged. He cursed fate and bemoaned his stupid life and idiotic fantasies he would never realize. Once again, he withdrew, bitterly resenting every weakness of his mother. She, though more forgetful, sensed the heaviness and spite of his spirit and wrote to his older sister for help.

The older sister arrived and confronted the now middle-aged man about his attitude. Crying, he confessed again the longer story—his longing, the refusal of fate to honor his wish.

The older sister sighed. "It's not fair that this burden fell on you. We can take our mother in. We'll move her to our place and sell the house, and you can be free."

But this made the man feel worse. He knew how much it would hurt and humiliate his mother to lose her home and her freedom. Deep within his heart, a clarity emerged. He loved his mother and wanted to be of service, but this unmet dream festered.

"I need to go and see the lights. If you could stay with her a few months, I can go and come back."

Saying this filled his spirit with vigor. All of life came into harmony for his desire. His siblings agreed to share the time with their mother while he traveled. The money procured transportation and all that was needed in his travel. Within a month, he was gone, and soon the lights glimmered green and bright before his eyes and he wept.

When he returned, the man was transformed. He was kind and attentive toward his mother, and at times he left to see other visions while his family helped. When his mother passed, he was beside her, and his heart broke with the gratitude of knowing he'd honored her wishes.

Now an older man, unencumbered and having fulfilled his fate, he decided his town was a wonderful home. It was a place his desires could take root within his dreams, from which he could adventure and then return to the familiar. So, he stayed into his old age, with joy.

This story is one illustration of the dance of destiny and fate, and one possibility of how that dance could have unfolded. When the man fell too much into the resignation of fate, a voice of destiny came in to remind him of his power. Yet within him was also a part that could joyfully accept the fate allotted to him, more so once he allowed it to be a choice.

EXERCISE

Encountering Destiny and Fate

Pick two days—or two weeks if you want to go deep—to try on the perspectives of destiny and fate. You could use the candle exercise at the beginning of the chapter to meet the twins and feel how it is to inhabit their bodies.

On the first day, before starting on the business of life, take a moment to imagine you can breathe in the energies of fate. As you breathe, allow the twin of fate to envelope you, suffuse your energy bodies, your physical body. Ask fate to show you how it is to walk in its world. As you go through your day, allow fate to show you how it is to live without agency, where even your thoughts are beyond your control. Keep breathing to reconnect to its being throughout the day, knowing this is an exercise. At the end of the day, thank the twin of fate and breathe into your core. As you exhale, imagine you can push out the energy of fate from the inside out.

The next day, similarly take time before getting started with your day to breathe in the energies of destiny. Allow the twin of destiny to saturate your being and show you how it is to walk in its world. As you go through the day, allow destiny to show you how it is to live when all that occurs is a direct response to your choices. Let it show you how your presence changes a room. The most subtle glance sets the trajectory of a conversation. Keep breathing to reconnect to its being throughout the day. At the end, thank the twin of destiny and breathe it out of your body, starting in your core and pushing its energy clear.

Journal about what you noticed in each experience. What felt useful about the perspective? What felt challenging about the perspective? How did others seem to change in relation to you based on the perspective you inhabited?

Going Deeper into Destiny

At its furthest edge, destiny is a path of radical self-responsibility. What will occur is a result of what we do, and we as workers of magic have the capacity to continually alter and refine the destiny of our paths. We still must live with the results of our actions. We cannot undo what has been done, and it is unclear how much we can influence the world after death; for simplicity's sake, let's assume there is a point when our role as characters in the story of the world ends. What happens to our legacy is carried forth in the destinies of those we have influenced. There are practitioners who believe the power of the magical will extends beyond the bounds of life. When I was a teenager, I came upon a strange interview between Christian television personality and exorcist Bob Larson and two people who were actively involved in the Temple of Set. One of the people was Zeena Schreck, daughter of Anton LaVey. Her assertion was that the power of will was so paramount that she believed she guided her parents to meet and procreate so that her soul could be born into her body and circumstances.[8] Practicing from this perspective deifies the personal will until it becomes a mystery unto ourselves. Our sovereignty is so profound that we create experiences for ourselves before we can be consciously aware of our own agency. Yet if our destiny is so powerfully determined

---

8. *Showdown with Satanism*, documentary, 1997. Produced by Bob Larson Ministries Video. Zeena has since renounced Satanism, Western occultism, and other magical "trends" as "not a viable route to freedom, liberation and enlightenment" per her website's frequently asked questions page https://www.zeenaschreck.com/general-info.html.

by our actions and character, how do we account for random accidents and acts of cruelty that befall the best among us and derail our plans?

From the perspective of destiny at its extreme, we manifested these misfortunes to teach ourselves to awaken more fully. Or our own weakness and insecurities produced these sufferings when we failed to claim our power over the chaos seeping into life. Taking either of these views as an empowering challenge spurs us to wake up and become more assertive with our power. At its best, destiny rouses us from feelings of powerlessness and walking through the world half-asleep. If we are suffering, it is on us to consider why we've created this suffering for ourselves and what we're going to do about it. Yet this perspective may also be incredibly cruel, belittling, and hurtful to share with a person in the midst of depression, great loss, or discouragement. They may hear this more as condemnation than encouragement. When we're hurting and need connection, compassion, and care, the "tough love" of destiny sounds like, "It's your fault, and you're on your own."

At its worst, destiny wraps us up into self-obsessed fantasies of power that pull us out of relationship with other people and the larger flow of God Herself. We withdraw attention from learning to work with those currents of connection, plowing forward in the most unskillful and obtuse ways. We center ourselves as the main character of the entire world's story and lose opportunities for intimacy and the profound teaching of humility. Our perceived power and aloneness may flood us with anxiety, causing us to obsess over every thought and instinct lest we betray ourselves, or may leave us wrapped in self-defeating, self-blaming stories when things don't go the way we want. None of us exist in isolation, and none of us are the solely all-powerful author of what happens. Thank the gods!

EXERCISE
Reflections of Destiny

Let's explore the useful qualities of destiny. When I want to practice with this perspective, I do reflective journaling on a recent setback, disappointment, or failure of action. The prompt I use is: "Why would I have created this experience for myself?" The goal is to go deeper than the self-defeating stories. What if there were good reasons for you manifesting this seemingly unwanted outcome? What if this outcome serves you in an important way? For example, if I want to get a new job but keep getting rejections, sitting with this question means daring to go deeper into possibilities. What if there was a good reason I was not manifesting a new job for myself? Is there a part of me undermining these opportunities to protect me from an obscure threat? Is there an opportunity I'm missing in my current job that's worth confronting?

Going Deeper into Fate

At its furthest edge, fate is the path of radical surrender. What will occur will occur no matter what you do about it. Fate may be written by the movement of the planets, the will of the gods, the economic changes wrought by climate or human behavior, or the cycles of history. We can also see an attitude of fatalism in those people who claim we are merely a product of our genetic programming or childhood experiences and condemned to live the life written for us. The illusion of freedom itself serves the inevitability of fate. How often have I tried to avoid conflict with people only to have my efforts become the cause of the conflict! One simple way to encounter fate and the limits of our power is to begin a sitting practice with the expectation that we'll be able to quiet our mind at once. Quickly it becomes clear how little control we have over our thoughts and feelings. Some of our behaviors, too, happen without our "will." Genetics, buried emotional pain, compulsive instincts, or the subtle manipulations of advertising and political propaganda drive and limit how we act. Our bodies grow ill, weak, and frail regardless of our will or greatest desires.

Practicing from this perspective offers a paradoxical liberation. A great deal of tension drains away when we give up our illusions of agency. We can start to witness ourselves with kindness and compassion. We don't have to waste energy wrangling intrusive thoughts and unwanted feelings or worry about the long-term consequences of our daily decisions. We can awaken internally and watch the unfolding of fate with curiosity, not taking life so personally. We could also practice from a perspective of surrendering to those beings who guide or write our fate, another act of will that requires presence. No longer struggling against what will happen anyway brings a softness and ease that lets things move more smoothly.

At its best, fate helps us accept what's outside of our power and be more present in the unfolding of life. It teaches us humility and an attitude of receptivity and listening. At its worst, fate renders us powerless, slack, and constantly victimized. We feel life is being done *to* us, all our suffering intended to harm us specifically. Or we may be unwilling to accept any responsibility for how we affect others. We give up too easily and quickly and see any setback as a sign that "the universe" is against what we want. The more we see and understand ourselves, the more potential power is available to us. By accepting our patterns and the larger non-negotiable influences of law, culture, and the limits of the physical world, we have more workable options.

EXERCISE
Reflections of Fate

When I want to practice taking on the perspective of fate,
I do reflective journaling on a recent experience that was
emotionally charged, for which I feel either extreme guilt
or a sense of great pride and accomplishment. The prompt
I use is: "What would it mean if this would have happened regardless of what I did?" The goal is not to fall into
cynical powerlessness but to reflect on what other forces
were involved in the experience. How did others participate? How did the environment, the day, the history, the
context influence what happened? How would I feel if I
did not bear sole responsibility?

The Peacock

The separation and honoring of the twins allows the peacock to
emerge. Whereas the twins are two opposing answers to a common
problem, the peacock is the brilliant solution in which the problem
dissolves. It is the synthesis that emerges from the polarization. The
peacock restores the wholeness of God Herself with the understanding earned from the experience of division and conflict. The peacock
does not intellectually seek a middle ground between the polarities,
nor does it force compromise where either of the twins must be
diminished. The peacock reconciles the twins by honoring what is
true and potent in each, allowing them to join in common cause.
Centered in our power, we acknowledge what is valid in the needs,
fears, and desires from these polarizations. That process catalyzes this
new expression that includes and transcends every part. The manner
in which the peacock manifests is unique, unexpected, surprising,
and profoundly *right*. We could never have imagined it before, but
once we step into it, it feels like it could have been no other way.

That is not to say it's always a joyful experience; it may be terrifying, it may be heartbreaking. But it still feels like what has to happen.

EXERCISE

Meeting the Peacock

Revisit the candle work from earlier in this chapter, but now add a fourth candle to represent the peacock. This candle could be any size or shape and the color could be gold, blue, green, or otherwise peacock-related.

Imagine the totality of space and time—it contains all that is and could be and yet is nothing of itself. Light the candle representing the star goddess, God Herself. Take up the candles of the twins and light each from the flame of the God Herself candle. Imagine what was nothingness becoming two, one bright and one dark. Meditate upon how the flame of the star goddess candle remains intact yet has also divided between these twins. As best as you are able—avoid burning yourself or lighting anything else aflame—bring the two flames of the twins' candles to the wick of the peacock candle, and let it catch. What was two becomes one.

Imagine the bright and dark twins joining together and blooming as beautiful feathers and a ferocious, serpentine neck with a piercing bird's face whose shriek makes the heavens shake. Meditate upon the journey of this flame that has moved between these candles and remains burning in each.

Evolution

The tension between destiny and fate enables us to evolve. Evolution is the compulsion to adapt to changing circumstances to ensure the best possible outcome for the survival of ourselves and our descendants. Evolution has been burdened with stories about superiority, but our adaptations are not necessarily superior to those of the mosquito's. Changing climates and cultures compel us to look at whether old ways of being are no longer working and cultivate what is necessary now and in the days to come. Our vitality drives us to continue to live, to neutralize old limitations with new possibilities. In this, the peacock is guide and mentor, engaging will and power to stay in active relationship, devotion, and dialogue with God Herself. Neither controls the other, but their relationship makes everything possible. The peacock does not wait for permission from God Herself to determine what they desire. They scream their desire into the black bowl of space; God Herself responds, and the peacock adapts.

So it is with slow magic. We spend years stuck, unable to make a hard choice, waiting for a sign to tell us what to do. Yet we have no clarity about what we want, so no sign could guide us. The path finds us when we step forward with intention. When we cast a spell, though we may not know how it will occur, our commitment and will make it possible for the path forward to appear. Yet we must change in this stepping forward. The path never appears as we imagine, and its demands will refine us. Old problems dissolve while surprising new problems emerge. We know, though we may forget to acknowledge, that any risk is easier when you have resources and support. Social status, community support, intergenerational wealth, a loving family, and robust social safety nets all allow embracing risk to be a thrilling adventure, rather than a reckless gamble with one's life and future. When working with slow magic, however, we are wise to remember that big, flashy, reckless acts are not always the move to make. Perhaps the work today is reaching out to have a meal with a new friend to build your web of community support; or to look for a job with health insurance; or to walk through your day with senses open, seeking new opportunity in the familiar.

The pressures of evolution require us to look at the truth of the desire, the desires within the desire. What we think we want to manifest may be a poor adaptation that will not weather the currents. To manifest anything of value tends to require the sacrifice of what felt comfortable and safe. Who we are today may not be a person who can experience that desire. That person needs to wilt and compost, so that the seeds of the future you can grow and flower. Find the moments in your life today where you feel the slightest hint of that desire, and bring your attention to it so it can grow.

EXERCISE
Divining the Next Step on the Path

Get your tarot cards (or your preferred divination tool). Clear a space and take three deep breaths. Call upon the wisdom of your divine nature and those spirits that love and aid you.

Draw one card for fate, and lay it on the left side, with the question, "What in my life do I need to accept as being beyond my power to influence?"

Draw one card for destiny, and lay it on the right side, with the question, "What in my life do I need to realize is within my power to influence?"

Then draw one card for evolution, and lay it in the center, with the question, "What is required of me to move toward my desire?"

Notice what arises. Vow to act on this guidance, even if in a small way, within the next day.

Chapter 3

STEPPING ONTO THE PATH

You may have a clear desire for your magic, or you may stress over knowing how to know what to want. The latter has been my problem. I coped with the not-knowing by consuming self-help books, therapy, workshops—lesson after lesson in the hopes I'd reach a point of "done-ness" when I could confidently go forth and manifest the dreams I now understood I had. There is no such moment of done-ness. No spirit comes forward to tell you that you've learned all the things and know with your true, authentic desire. Authentic desire transforms as we live into it. Meanwhile the tasks of life must be tended to, and there's no benefit to cordoning contemplative work off from the mundane. Engaging both together benefits us. The work of this book will support you in building confidence in your practice. Confidence is not an absence of doubt or fear. Confidence does not mean clinging to certainty and never reevaluating your beliefs and desires. Confidence is the attitude of knowing you can get through anything, that you matter, and thus you can approach your work with genuine curiosity and a willingness to listen.

Setting Your Aim

Think of slow magic as firing an arrow over a great distance. Should you aim too low, your projectile is likely to hit dirt before it gets where you want it to be. Archers aim high so that the velocity of their shot counteracts the drag of gravity. The arrow arcs upward across distance until its upward momentum is depleted, and then it continues to cover distance while descending toward the target. When I do therapeutic work with people in their early twenties, I notice how often they freeze when it's time to aim high. There's this realization that they could achieve so much if they committed to it, yet there is hesitation coming from uncertainty about what they want, fear of wasting potential by following the wrong path, or worry over making a mistake that will forever foreclose all other possibilities. Such caution inhibits any kind of action, ironically contributing to mistakes and wasted time. What these young adults (and, frankly, some much older adults) need to learn is that missteps and mistakes are inevitable and important. They're not experiences to fear.

Accepting that wasted time and mistakes are a part of learning frees us up to play. We can try things and see what works, what we liked, and what we absolutely hated. When there's a failure, we can take what we learned and try again with more maturity and wisdom. "But not all of us have room to fail," you might think. It is true that those with a great deal of wealth, power, or social support have more cushion to weather shocks and setbacks against damage to their future. Some of us feel constantly on the precipice, having never felt we could rely on that kind of support or only knowing abandonment at times of need. It's fully understandable that taking risks would be too terrifying to allow. Indeed, words like "commitment" and "wanting" may feel too charged. Curiosity is a gentler space to start our magic, and it can take us far. What sounds interesting? What do I want to learn?

Approaching with this energy allows magic to bloom without the pressure and force of needing it to become anything in particular. Instead of needing to know we're on track to manifest a long-term marriage—making every first date laden with expectation and pressure—we could approach every encounter with curiosity about where it will lead. Perhaps this manifests a nice first date that turns into a friendship. Perhaps it manifests a nice date that leads to another, and then another, and eventually you and the other person decide marriage feels like the right next step. Curiosity, experimentation, and exploration allows our work to be about gathering more information and investing slowly. Where you are right now is completely okay, and you do not have to stay here. You have all you need within you to open up to your calling and purpose and work your will. There is nothing to fix, but effort is required. If you want to get strong or maintain your strength, you need to move your body and experience discomfort. But it is wise to find the edge you want to grow and start working it.

EXERCISE

From Where You Stand

Consider one of your biggest dreams, your long-term goals, or an experience you're curious to have. Take a blank piece of paper and write that desire at the top. Beneath it, make a list of all the things that you know need to happen between where you are now and that point. If there are steps you don't understand or don't know enough about to know where to begin, include that on your list—learning these things is a step. Once you've listed everything that needs to happen, look for the task that is the easiest for you to reach today. Sign up for a class, request a book from the library, or reach out to a friend or mentor who might have advice for you. Or take the next indicated step.

If you like, you can keep this paper with your goals and steps to return to and refine on your journey or use it as a magical object. If the paper and ink won't harm the earth, you could bury it in your yard or in a sacred place to plant the seed of your future self. You could fold it into a paper airplane and cast it onto the wind to connect with the allies you'll need. You get the idea.

EXERCISE
Toward What You Seek

When working with a big, ambitious goal, you can set your aim the highest and do spellwork for the ultimate aim. You can also aim lower, toward the smaller goals within that larger one. It's not about doing the same spell over and over, which conveys insecurity and a shakiness of will. Instead it's about keeping engaged with your magic and the flow of God Herself, steering your boat through the currents and making adjustments as necessary. Reflect on what it is you are looking for or want to move toward when setting your aim. If all you can think of is what you do *not* want to happen or want to avoid, your intention will be too rooted in control, fear, or anger to be effective. Do you want to be defined by what you hate and oppose? Do you want to spend your energy tracking marginal wins and losses? Do you want to be brittle in relationships? There are times when it is necessary to set up the shields and point our weapons at those who oppose us, but when we live in that kind of magic, all we perceive are enemies.

A truly ambitious goal transforms ourselves and our living conditions by necessity. The slow magic approach assumes that if we could have what we wanted right now, we would. If we do not, then our current conditions are not favorable to that desire sprouting and blooming. Setting magical intention into motion initiates the changes that make your conditions more fertile for your desire. It is a crucial phase in magical work. The more I practice crafting spells, the more I find they begin to "work" as soon as I have a clear intention before I've executed the spell. Setting an intention aligns the human, animal, and god souls within us through language, resonance, and symbolism. One approach favors the human soul, using language to name a clear and precise statement of intention. Another approach favors the playful animal soul, gathering symbols and ingredients that feel resonant with the intention. We will go deeper into both approaches.

Statement of Intent

When drafting a statement of intention, begin by drawing upon all the brainstorming, divination, and inspiration you've received that led to you naming this desire. Much of the work of this book contributes to the material you need. You could begin by writing out a narrative of what you want the result to look like. Once complete, try to distill the narrative into one sentence written in the present tense in an active voice. The active voice is a literary term for a sentence in which the subject is doing the verb: "I cooked a black bean burger." The passive voice is written as though things are being done to the subject: "A black bean burger was made for me." In this you may hear echoes of the twins of destiny and fate—either we are agents in the world or we are recipients of a mysterious force.

The active voice energizes that sense of will and vitality that I want in doing magical work.

To call in more of our holistic, instinctive self, consider using verbs that feel metaphorical and enlivening. Consider the difference between "I feel happier" and "I seduce joy." There's nothing wrong with a plain statement of intent, but there's an extra burst of life force in these dynamic verbs. The present tense is another stylistic choice that adds more vitality to an intention. We write as though the result is already occurring. It is inevitable, even if set in the future. To me, this mindset evokes the mystery of magic, that all I desire is located within me. Including a deadline for manifestation is useful. A vague or unnamed timeline is one way we aim too low and give our intention drag, sending it into the dirt. Were I to summon brownies to me at a time of the universe's choosing, who knows how long I will need to wait. Perhaps the brownies will appear when I no longer want them…better to call upon brownies for dessert tonight! Examples: For a love spell: "On February 14, 2025, I kiss my beloved in our shared home." For employment: "By March 2024, I work at a job that pays me enough to pay my bills and allows me time to take a vacation." For health goals: "Before June, I meet with a doctor who listens to me, takes me seriously, and gives me the tools to manage my chronic illness."

The only goals for which you should disregard deadlines are those you want to persist and endure, such as magic that changes conditions. I recall an instance when I was feeling drained by my smartphone and social media. I created an intention to install a better relationship into myself and made it into a sigil I could see every time I unlocked my phone. Examples: For effective communications, "My words soar with ease and grace to find what they need." For prosperity, "Money flows to me whenever I have need of it." For a happy home, "My house abounds with safety and love."

Resonant Assemblage

This process is more intuitive and playful, and a spell on its own. It's my favorite way of doing magic, inviting creative chaos and revelations from the deeper parts of ourselves that come forward in sensation and symbol. It puts those logical, controlling parts of the self into the audience with a bucket of popcorn to watch and see what unfolds. This approach marries will with surrender to what we receive from spirits without and within. In brief, this method is about gathering objects, images, and symbols that resonate with the qualities we want to invite in, expel, or transform. We still enter into this process with a basic sense of what we're aiming to do, but the language of the intention would be far more spacious and undefined. Perhaps it is more a single word or phrase than a complete statement: "Calmness." "Protection." "Wealth."

One beloved example is collage work. When we gather pieces of imagery that feel exciting, intriguing, or relevant and then assemble them on a page based on what feels right, we invite in the qualities of these images and let our instinctive soul show us how these things relate. Surprising connections and conjunctions emerge. The collage teaches us a great deal about our desire every time we look at it. Another example is along the lines of the jar spell or the charm bag, in which we gather whatever herbs, stones, symbols, or objects seem to go together. These are like a good hearty stew where the ingredients simmer and come together into a unique and nourishing meal. These spells tend to be more portable, so we can carry the spell with us or put it in places that might otherwise be inconvenient—like at our work station.

Crafting Your Spell

Magic is and has been practiced in almost every class, every historical era, every group. Calling these diverse practices "magic" might offend some of these groups, but we see the parallels of using spiritual power to make physical changes. Enslaved people in the United States used roots, herbs, and whatever else was at hand to fix their spouses in place when their enslavers threatened to separate the families. Royal courts employed astrologers and magicians to advise and influence the leadership in taking actions that would best serve their kingdoms. When I was growing up, my Catholic grandmother told stories of natural healers born with a caul over their face who were able to cure warts and burns through strange rituals with pennies. All this is to say that magic is always at hand and could be as complex as you'd like or as simple as you need. There have been times I have invested in components and tools that stretched my budget because it stretched me and compelled me to take my magic more seriously. And I have also done satisfying work with a pen and a piece of paper. In spellcraft, we take what is common and make it sacred, imbued with will and desire and the forces of those beings who offer aid and challenge. With this making sacred, what was nothing special becomes the vehicle for influencing the deeper self and the outer forces of the world toward our end.

There are numerous ways of doing spellwork, and I enjoy learning different approaches. I went through a sigil phase, a poppet phase, then a candle phase, then I was into jar spells. When I want to learn a new kind of spellwork, I'll make up reasons to do magic. Now I let my animal soul lead me to the spell approach that feels right for the intention at hand. Having a physical anchor for the spell's intention helps us to remember we want our results to manifest in the physical world. The nature of the object informs what it manifests. Think metaphorically. Lighting a candle or a lamp could bring clarity and illumination, or it could devour and consume. Charging a stone brings its qualities of density, weight, and solid-ity to a working, and each stone offers its unique flavor of energy. Spray bottles with blessed water and resonant herbs and oils fill the room with their qualities, changing the climate. Consider also the process of the spell. When you put things into a jar or a bottle, is it a container for things to stew and cook? Is it a prison? A magnet? A seed? None of these answers are wrong, but each changes the engagement.

You can certainly get started right away with what you've got. But if you want to go more deeply into practice, take time to purify the materials so they are open to your intent. Cleanse them of old intentions they served, or of other people's energies upon them. Rosemary and lavender grow in my yard, so each fall I've begun harvesting branches of both to dry and bind into a bundle that I can use for smoke cleansing. When blessing a spell object, I cense it with the smoke and pray for the dispersal of what is no longer needed.

The spell is the process of imbuing this material with your intention. You could speak that intention into it or breathe your desire into it. When possible, I mark the object with my intention. My preferred way of integrating the intention is to convert my written statement into a sigil and then draw or carve it onto the object. This process deepens the connection between my rational and instinctive souls, converting language into pure symbol.[9] If you are in relationship with spirits, it's also beneficial to call upon the ones favorable to this work and ask for their blessing and

---

9. There are numerous methods for creating sigils, and there are online sigil generators if you're not interested in the nuts and bolts. If you'd like to learn more, here are three recommendations:

Ivo Dominguez, Jr., *Practical Astrology for Witches and Pagans* (Red Wheel/Weiser, 2016).

T. Thorn Coyle, *Sigil Magic: For Writers and Other Creatives* (PF Publishing, 2015).

Laura Tempest Zakroff, *Sigil Witchery: A Witch's Guide to Making Magic Symbols* (Llewellyn Publications, 2018).

support. Listen for what they might need you to do. Try to imagine how those spirits are supporting you and imbuing the object with their essence. Then it is time to charge the spell. This is the moment of transmutation from common to sacred, enlivening the spell and investing it with spirit. Your witnessing, presence, and aliveness make this change possible. You could gaze upon the spell in meditation until you sense it is complete. You could dance, laugh, move, or make love to yourself to raise power and send that life force into the spell. You could call up the powers of earth and sky and breathe it into your spell.

Finally, you need to do something with it. This step is as important as all that's come before. You now have a sacred embodiment of your will and desire. What you do to or with it shapes how its work will unfold. Will it be gradual or sudden? Explosive or soft? Are you breaking, planting, burying, or building? Is this going to be a fence, a pot, an arrow, a snare, or a falcon seeking prey? These kinds of dynamic symbols bring vitality and form to the work. Our parts that feel alone can relax into the knowing that we've crafted a helper to do the work for us, in the way it was intended. Let the magic come to you as you walk your path. Eventually, this magic will reach its fruition, or a point in which it must be dissolved so you can move forward. We will discuss that process toward the end of this book.

Daily Practice

Daily magical practice is another method of cultivating will, tending relationships with the currents of God Herself, and enhancing your spellwork. Making a promise to oneself and following through brings confidence that leads to bigger commitments. Breaking down big works into daily practices also helps build momentum and steadiness. It would be unlikely to manifest a thriving garden

in a day, but if you dedicated a portion of time each day to cultivating the land, eventually you'd have your desire. Warm, pleasant
days where you have free time and abundant energy may find you
putting in more effort, while on other days you might find it wise
to do a little, and let yourself and the land rest. You can be gentle
with yourself, abbreviating or missing a day of practice when illness or other circumstances become unmanageable—but return to
your routine as soon as you can.

Below is a simple way to begin a daily practice if you do not
have one. This method offers a structure to check in and deepen
your intimacy with your souls. I include a version of mindfulness
meditation. Those of us with a little knowledge and training may
think our minds need to be silent and empty to be effective medi-
tators, but it turns out that attachment to "needing to be silent" is
another part of self to accept in spacious witness. Witnessing helps
us know ourselves better and connect with the part of us that is
separate from the contents of our thoughts, feelings, and instincts.
Connecting to this witness is of itself profoundly transformative
and expansive. The practice concludes with soul alignment. Alignment is a way of deepening the relationship between all of our
parts, improving their harmonious connection, and creating more
safety and support for our magic. We connect ourselves to god
soul, the divine part of us that is our aspect of God Herself. We
will go even deeper into god soul in chapter 9, but it is a worthy
ally with its well of endless compassion and patience, and safety
when our parts want to lead our magic to tricky places.

EXERCISE
Morning Check-In and Soul Alignment

What appears here is an abbreviated version of my daily
practice with room for expansion. Although you start with

five minutes, you may choose to add more time. I usually do twenty to thirty minutes a day. Occasionally I've sat for longer periods. Occasionally the best I can do is five minutes.

Find a place where you will be safe and undisturbed. Let people know not to interrupt you. The aim is to be fully present for this time, so minimize distractions as much as possible. I set a timer on my phone so that I do not need to check the clock, and I turn my notifications off to avoid being interrupted or tempted to check it. Find a posture you can hold for five minutes—standing, walking, kneeling, or sitting cross-legged are all acceptable. If you need to lie down and can do so without falling asleep, do what you've got to do; however, an active and engaged posture supports presence in meditation. Reach through the top of your head upward and the tip of your tailbone downward. Roll your shoulders front to back and let them rest slightly behind you. Lift up your head and settle it back on your neck, chin pointed slightly downward. Let this be both engaged and soft, relaxing any clenched muscles.

Let your breathing slow down. Notice what comes up in you as you do this. Your whole being is a theater, and there is an observing part of you that can watch the play of thoughts, emotions, and sensations in your body. When you notice your mind is preoccupied, acknowledge it as a part of yourself that is trying to accomplish a task for you. Invite it to sit with you in meditation. If the part refuses, accept it and bring your attention back to your breathing without getting further involved. Continue doing this for as many parts as you notice.

You do not have to "try" to quiet your mind. Only see if you can sense the calm, clear spaciousness that is present in the capacity to witness your mind, and invite your parts to join you in it. Most of our parts are unaware or mistrustful of this underlying consciousness, and we are often so fused with one or two parts that feel like "us" that we do not recognize the spaciousness in which these parts exist. Breath calms the body, and breath also reminds us of air. Air exists all the time in the space around us, but we may forget it in our attention to the dogs barking, the messy dishes, the endless stream of texts. But we breathe in and exhale air, and air remains what it is.

Once the time you've set aside is complete, it is time to align your souls. Breathe in until your belly is full, then hold for a few beats. Imagine there is a bowl in your belly that you can fill with this breath and life force. As you exhale, do not empty this bowl, but keep breathing in more life force until it is overflowing. Imagine that there is a channel between your belly and heart, and that overflowing life force naturally and easily rises to begin to fill the bowl inside your heart. Continue breathing in this way until belly and heart are overflowing. Imagine another channel joining your heart and the center of your head and that overflowing life force naturally and easily rises to begin to fill your skull. Continue breathing in this way until your belly, heart, and head are full.

Imagine there is a sphere floating above you, containing your divinity. Tilt your head back and forcefully exhale your overflowing aliveness up to connect all of your centers to this facet of your soul. Pause and notice what happens in you as this sphere receives and redistributes the energy. Say a prayer honoring your divinity and inviting in its guidance and wisdom. Here is one of mine:

Welcome, you flame of living spirit.
For you, my soul is teeming ocean,
love without limit, encircling all.
May this practice be a tower
upon which you can bear witness
and guide the lost in seeking home.

The Rose of Desire

When you're feeling stuck, lost, or in a bad place, the Rose of Desire offers a path and a structure of daily practice to get you in motion. The Rose of Desire is a tarot spread that came to me when I was working on befriending desire. I did not know how to know what I wanted. Naming a concrete desire stirred up my parts—a part of me was afraid of getting it wrong, another part felt confused by the material world and wanted to check out, and other parts shut down desire to keep me safe. Using tarot as a vehicle helped these parts be more open to exploring. The symbolism offered a container while remaining open to multiple possibilities of manifestation. We can feel a card like the Star is calling to us without having a clear vision of what it would look like in life. As I've worked more with tarot, I do find it speaks to me of different ways to practice with the energies of the cards. A card may offer a provocative question to journal. It may offer a challenging practice, such as going and risking honesty with a person. It may say to calm down and take a day off.

Tarot is primarily a tool of divination, whose symbolism provides language for comprehending the subtle forces moving in your life and helps you receive information and guidance from the guides and spirits that aid you. The information shows where you're headed if you stay on this path, and where you might change your path. You can also deploy tarot for spellwork, laying out an intentional spread with each card chosen to represent the forces you are calling in for manifestation. Rather than leaving it up to chance, you craft the spread that represents your will. The Rose of Desire synthesizes these two approaches. We begin with an act of self-awareness and will to discern where we are, and leave space for guidance from the other realms. Then we engage our will in following the path laid out. Of all things, this kind of work with tarot teaches me the most about the principle that when we risk stepping out into the unknown with will, the path finds us.

EXERCISE
The Rose of Desire

Take stock of yourself in this moment—your challenges and gifts, where you feel stuck, what is unwanted, and what is working. Look through your preferred tarot deck and pull out the card that best represents this moment for you. Place that on a large surface. This will be card 1. Then contemplate where you'd like to be in two weeks. Think about how you'd like to feel in your life, what movement you'd like to see. Look through the deck again and notice how you feel toward each card. Find a card that feels like it best represents where you would like to be. If you don't know, that is okay—instead pick a card that is the most appealing to you, the most intriguing, or the most stabilizing. Place your choice to the right of the first card with a fair amount of room. If you look through the deck and still feel stuck on what card to choose for 14, then leave it empty for now. Shuffle the deck, inviting in the spirits or guide you'd like to aid you in the journey from 1 to

14. Starting to the left of card 1, lay out twelve cards in a counterclockwise spiral, out and down from #1 and arcing back around, up, and into 14 as the center of the spread. If you were unable to choose a card for 14, lay out the whole sequence from your deck and see what is given to you.

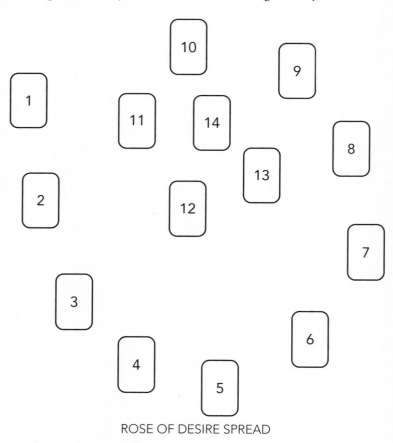

ROSE OF DESIRE SPREAD

Take out a journal and document the reading. Card 1 represents the conditions you want to escape, or transform. Card 14 represents your desire, what you are seeking. Cards 2 through 13 represent the path of transformation to follow. They also represent the days to come. Card 1 is today, and card 14 is two weeks from now. The reading shows you what to do during the intervening days. Ask each card for guidance about what is needed each day to engage in transformation. Listen for specific practices—questions for reflection, contemplations on yourself and your surroundings, or actions you can take. Let the cards teach you how to engage each day so that the energies of transformation can come through and help you move toward your desire. For the next thirteen days, act on this guidance. Take it one day and one card at a time. Do your best to honor what was offered to you, but if you miss a day, let it go and commit to returning to the guidance of the following day. When you get to day 14, reflect on how the energy of the card you chose is being expressed. Does it feel strong or weak? Do you feel the seeds of it within you or does it feel in full flower?

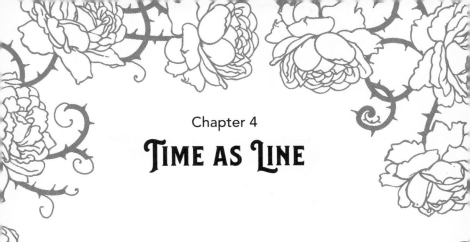

Chapter 4

TIME AS LINE

Having a sense of time—of a past, a present, and a future—is a deeply important psychological foundation, without which we have nothing to stand upon. This truth revealed itself to me during the intense period of isolation after the outbreak of COVID-19. I lived in Washington state, where we were one of the strictest states in following social distancing, masking, and the shutdown of social spaces. I affirmed those actions and avoided close contact with anyone outside of my household. As a mental health therapist living through this alongside my clients, I had a unique opportunity to observe shared experiences. Those early months teemed with sorrow, anger, and the disorientation of abruptly losing our futures. So many of us entered the year with exciting plans and hopes to be daring, break patterns, and try new ways to make our life better. The pandemic and lockdowns were like a cosmic hand shoving us back into place, forcing us to cancel and indefinitely postpone those plans. It was too easy to let this feed the harshest stories of fate: "This is what I get. I'm never allowed to have what I want."

Crisis and great stress offers a measure of how much you've grown by showing how far you regress. Old patterns of coping bring comfort even when they cause other kinds of misery. Stress and emotional overload tends to overwhelm the newer habits and send our scared parts back to what is at least predictable. Thus, in the early phase of the isolation period, I observed a common tendency to retreat into the familiarity of old vices, old patterns, and old ways of being. This retreat emerged in response to grief, but in particular to what I've come to think of as the horror of the eternal present. With no certainty for the future and the anxious terror of catching a mysterious virus with the risks of death or long-term disability, many of us spent hours and days in a sort of stupor that felt both endless and fleeting. While there was no shortage of memes and social media exhortations to make the most of this moment with ambitious, transformative projects and hobbies, I would say it was the exception rather than the rule of how people coped in the first year. With nothing solid to plan around, we lived in the horror of the eternal present. We could hope and believe things would change, but we did not know when that day would come. For a while, we lived outside of the continuity of time. Without a future, there was nothing to grow toward, which made motivation and focus hard to muster.

Slow magic helped me reanchor to time, as tentative as it was. Every New Year's Eve, I create a magical collage to represent the energies I want to embody and experience for the upcoming year. Occasionally I would pick a single word to orient around. For 2020, I chose the word "expansive." My expansive collage was unusually dense and multilayered, a spiral atop a labyrinth atop a tree. I included a quote attributed to Jung: "No tree, it is said, can grow to heaven unless its roots reach down to hell."[10] What I imagined would be a year of taking up more space, dreaming bigger, and breaking down my perceived limits—growing up to heaven— turned out to be a year of expanding inward and downward, sinking my roots all the way to hell.

---

10. Carl Gustav Jung, *Aion: Researches into the Phenomenology of the Self*, trans. and ed. Gerhard Adler (Routledge, 1981), 43.

Practicing growth and expansion even in this time kept me connected to magic. I needed to grieve the future I'd envisioned for myself. I wrote down all my plans for the year, my hopes for the future, the dreams that had to be postponed—and burnt them in a ritual fire. For a time, parts of me wanted to close myself off to desire to avoid more grief and loss. The greatest danger I feared was false hope—to keep expecting it to end and be repeatedly crushed with this disappointment felt dangerous. Though all I wanted was to slumber until it was safe to reemerge, the intention of being expansive kept nudging me awake. Even in times of great constriction when gains are hard to make, exerting ourselves slows the creep of decline. We lose less than we otherwise might.

One day, seeing my own therapist, I felt a part of me beginning to dream about one day traveling again. My heart ached as a green sprout of desire fought against everything that wanted it to stay hidden. Not a hope for life as it had been before, but a hope there would be more life to come. A life in which pleasure, adventure, and connection would be possible. This kind of hope is a lantern in times of turmoil. We can hold it before us and let its light find the next steps on the path, though the storm itself rages and consumes and it seems impossible to believe it will ever end. As of this writing, the storm begun by that pandemic has not yet ended. And, at the same time, my hope lit the path toward all those joys of life I craved I'd find again and more than I'd imagined for myself.

Slow magic calls us into relationship with the depths of time. With schedules and alarms and deadlines pulling us ever forward, we tend to live on time's surface. The busyness of days threatens to overwhelm us when we try to engage magical work. We may rejoice in the passage of time when it closes the gap between ourselves and the weekend. We may fear the passage of time as it threatens us with the end of our days. Adversary or lover, time walks with us. We can make it our ally. In the next three chapters, we will explore our relationship with time, turning back to the divine twins and the peacock to show us three facets of magical time: the line, the cycle, and the spiral. We begin with linear time.

The Line

The geometrical archetype of the line is one continuous path with no beginning or ending, never intersecting with itself or looping back and retracing its movement. On earth, however, a line is a finite streak between two points, beginning and moving forward until its termination. Our lifespans are one such line, a path between birth and death measured by the clock and calendar. When we exalt the line, we tend to map it to stories of progress and decadence that have characterized Western thinking since at least the Enlightenment. In the myth of progress, our species began in ignorance and primitive origins and is moving ever-toward greater complexity, success, and prowess, typically represented by technological growth and scientific insight. We are smarter, healthier, wealthier, more virtuous, better informed. There are ongoing societal problems that need to be solved, but increased wisdom and technology will fix them. The shadow of progress is decadence and decline. In this myth, we drift further and further away from who we're supposed to be. We grow unhealthier, more dependent upon technologies that sap our freedom and vitality, further away from true virtue, more disconnected, more hostile toward each other. All societal problems are signs of this decline, and continuing on this path will be catastrophic. We should all return to some way of living that is in the past, but most people are too lost to know it.

Increasingly I find myths of progress and decline to be unhelpful distortions of how social change happens. For every loss there is gain, and our innovations and radical solutions create new problems. Yet the line has a use for assessing how our work is helping or hindering us, and myths of progress certainly offer us tools of measurement. One of our most revered and feared lines is that of the stock market. We watch it with anxious fervor, anticipating whether it will continue to climb or drop precipitously, and use that to assess our wealth and security. In linear time, the cycle is our great enemy. The great capitalist dream of unfettered growth and eternal expansion persists though we know it to be impossible. Contractions are inevitable, limits inescapable. We talk about being stuck in cycles we cannot escape as though those cycles arrest our progress or distract us from the path we're supposed to take. When we think we're adventuring into the unknown territory of progress, we find ourselves pulled backward into familiar habits and once again trace familiar territory. Truly the line of life is more of a meander, and we can always invite fresh energy into the tip of our movement. If we revisit old territory, we can enter it with fresh perspective invigorated by our journey and see if there's progress to be had even in the most intractable of problems. Linear time offers us wisdom for our magical work: the past shapes the future; the future guides the present.

The Past Shapes the Future

What we've experienced in the past shapes our capacity to imagine the future. While our capacity for learning and memory helps us to avoid reexperiencing danger and harm, it also makes us likely to only look for those risks and fail to recognize opportunities. Our understandings of personal and collective history form a lattice around the imagination, like a tomato cage, both enabling and containing growth. Should we dare to imagine a bold, different future for ourselves and do magic toward it, we'll feel the pinch of those old understandings in fear, anxiety, anger, and resistance to change. If all we've known is ease and privilege, we may avoid discomfort even if it leads to power. If all we've known is denial and deprivation, we may mistrust and refuse abundance when it shows up in life. We may even experience resistance from the stories and burdens of our ancestors, passed from generation to generation.

EXERCISE
Unearthing the Influences of the Past

One convenient way to explore this principle is to look at patterns from our families and our childhood. Take time, in whatever way feels right to you—journaling, voice dictation, making art, talking to a trusted friend or counselor—to reflect on the following questions: What was a normal day for your family? Was there a lot of laughter and humor? Was there often anger and fighting? Was there a lot of talking or very little? How many parents did you grow up with? Who worked, and where did they work? Did you eat as a family? Who cooked and cleaned? Did your parents tell you about their problems? Ask for your advice? Did you ever feel like you had to parent your parents? Did you feel like you could spend time with friends when you wanted? Did you feel encouraged to pursue your interests, or were other things more important?

Write about any or all of these questions and any further details that feel relevant to how your family operated. This was normal for you. Take a day to let these answers rest. When you're ready, review what you've written and continue to this reflection: When was the first time that you learned that what was normal for you wasn't normal for everyone else? What was it like to discover that other people had different childhoods, different experiences of family and parenting? Were there experiences you envied? Experiences that disturbed you?

Take another day or so to let this rest. When you are ready, finish with this reflection: When you reread what you wrote about your childhood normal, does any of it look like how you live today? Does your work, home, or relationship mirror any of your parents'? When you reread what you learned from seeing other people's families and childhood, does any of that look like how you live today? Have you integrated other possibilities of work, home, and relationship into your life?

Outdated Stories

We develop stories of the past when we're young that often persist in us though other parts grow older and wiser. A horrible accident at the age of five may result in a story of, "I'm bad and dangerous," when an adult mind would be able to clearly see there is no possible way for the child to be responsible. Yet that painful story lies in wait to be set off by the events of daily life. No matter how many corrective stories we've lain atop that underlying one, there's still a part of us that responds with tremendous shame and terror whenever it looks like we've caused harm. Or, it's just as possible that we avoid any risks because of this deep fear.

During the early days of COVID-19, I gravitated toward isolation because loneliness was my normal as a kid. Being without people would be easy for me, I thought. It was almost an unconscious assumption rather than a choice I made: of course I'll be alone and pass the time reading books and entertaining myself, that is familiar to me. But then I started to notice myself sliding further into depression and intense anxiety, which would be alleviated whenever we did leave the house to do an outdoor hangout with friends. Depression had also been my childhood norm, but this experience gave me a surprising new understanding: I was depressed because I was lonely. Now it seems obvious and silly that I'd missed it, but my young story had been that it was my depression that made me unable to connect and was the cause of my loneliness. In my professional life, I'd become familiar with the work of John Cacioppo, whose research showed that chronic loneliness tends to cause anyone experiencing it to be more withdrawn, more sensitive to rejection, less likely to reach out for the connection they crave.[11] It wasn't until the pandemic that I connected that to my own experience and could rewrite my story—that loneliness was a cause of depression and they could reinforce each other. With this clarity, it became apparent that I needed people, and I needed to make the effort to reach out to friends even more so when parts of me wanted to withdraw.

To shape a new future, we have to transform the past. Bringing our divine, conscious, living presence into relationship with that old pain supports it in releasing the suffering and rewriting the story. Until we do that, we may continue to live out the old story in our behavior and how we interpret what's happening around us. Our roots dig deep into the past, deeper than our own personal history, and are enlivened with the burdens and blessings of our ancestors and history. Our branches want to stretch up and out into the vast future. But when our roots are blocked and limited in their growth, we aren't able to expand into the sky. Our roots get blocked by being unable to imagine other possibilities and by fear and constriction. Even if we hate our past or where we've come from, it is familiar, and the familiar tends to be far more comforting than the risk of trying a different way. Instead of hating ourselves for this tendency, it is wiser to turn toward that fear and honor its innate desire for our safety and wellness.

---

11. John Cacioppo and William Patrick, *Loneliness: Human Nature and the Need for Social Connection* (W. W. Norton & Company, 2008), 3–19.

When we turn toward these older forces, their initial answers may be upsetting or offensive to us. These protective forces have been at it for so long, with so little support, that their messages to us feel abusive, ugly, or disturbing; other parts of us would rather they went away. These remind me of the robots in science fiction stories who exist under the directive to protect humans from harm but observe the harm humans do to themselves and conclude they must become tyrants to fulfill their mission. Good intentions become distorted and cruel. We can say no to the cruelty while still honoring the goodness of the intention, and in this work I find things tend to go better when we do. These forces respond to our love and admiration, which breaks the spell of their cruelty and reconnects them to their initial longing to love and support us.

EXERCISE
Befriending the Past

Consider your intention or a change you'd like to make in your life path. Draw a picture representing your intention to keep in front of you while you slow your breathing down and let your body settle. Imagine yourself as a great tree and the intention you hold resting in the middle of your trunk, wanting to stretch upward and outward. Ask to follow the energy of this intention into your roots. Ask this root to show you what happened in your life that was the seed of this desire. Wait for an answer to come.

Once you have your answer, ask the root what has prevented you from manifesting this desire in your life up until now. Breathe and try to witness what arises, whether it's a series of memories, a sensation, a story, or an intense part of you. Ask this root what it needs to support you in manifesting this desire now. Listen for an answer, whether it makes sense or not. If the answer is one you cannot or will not do, ask it, "What's important about this? What is beneath this?" Keep going until you find what you can do that will help this older force be on your side. Make a commitment that you can keep, and then add a symbol of this commitment to the picture of your intention.

The Future Guides the Present

Our present moment actions respond to the future we believe we will have. If you imagine that your future will be the same as your past, then your present behavior will be a continual re-enactment. Should we want magic and transformation, however, I offer this equation as a map to where you can change your destiny. Once you've rewritten the limiting stories of the past, you free up the future for new possibilities. Returning to my experience of the pandemic, my darkest days found me fixating on visions of a desolate, doomed future. It was easy to do. Those years were apocalyptic. Not only did we have a global disease we did not understand, isolation from each other, and the civil unrest of both anti-lockdown protests and anti-racist protests spurred by high-profile cases of police brutality, but we had the uncertainty of long-term unemployment. We had a government warring with itself and a president whose behavior was impulsive, unpredictable, and instinctively driven to maintain a level of chaos and tension. We had wildfires that caused, where I lived, days of smoke so thick and noxious that stepping outside and breathing the air unfiltered was worse for your health than hunkering down inside.

In my fixations, I imagined future worst-case scenarios: environmental, social, and political collapse. No clean water, no fresh food in the grocery stores, gangs on the street aligned with their own interests and free to use violence. Civil war. The further I went into seeing this fantasy as prophecy, the more I spent time reading about extreme political movements, posting cynical and despairing comments on social media, preparing my survival kit if we needed to flee the city, and generally sitting around feeling powerless and despondent.[12] One day I watched myself in this state and had the thought: *If this stuff doesn't happen, I'll have wasted so much of my life worrying about it.* The thought showed me that a part of me hoped these things would happen to validate how much I worried about them. I saw further how this fantasy lulled me into complacent, self-righteous, cynical surrender. I have a dear friend who does admirable, daunting activism in prison abolition with a relentless, stubborn form of hope that keeps them persevering. When I shared my despair about the future and admired their ability to hold hope, they responded, "There is no other option." The words were cold water to my fevered imagination. For my friend, living into a bleak and hopeless future is unacceptable, so they choose instead to keep fighting for their ideals and aspirations. I could follow their example, investing my attention into a better future. I could stop feeding my paralyzing fear fantasy and focus on exercise, prayer, meditation, work, and connecting to my family and community. Even if collapse is inevitable, these efforts matter. Life continues through the worst moments of human history.

Our expectations of the future tend to inform how we react to what's happening in the moment. When I have conflict with people, I used to immediately assume they would write me off, ridicule me, or shut me down. Assuming this future, it made sense to avoid dealing with them or trying to make my problems unimportant so I didn't have to face them. But now when I catch myself living that imagined future, I take a breath and remember times when conflict brought me closer to the people I love. Then I try

---

12. Preparing a survival kit was a constructive use for this anxiety. I found my terrified parts felt calmer when I took them seriously and came up with plans for those scenarios.

to live into that future—saying what I need to say and seeing how they respond. Even if it's hard to imagine a different future, we could try going in with curiosity to see if our assumptions end up coming true, or if life turns out to be an unexpected adventure. When we can desire a new future, we find its seeds in the present moment and nurture them with attention. As you imagine a future self who is bold, daring, and courageous, look for moments of courage and daring in your day to day. Seek opportunities for courage and then look at what gets in the way—go back to our work with the roots. Remember that growth is vulnerable and gradual. In springtime, established pine trees and shrubs show their growth in the fresh greenness of the needles stretching out from what has been established. That greenness is tender, still adjusting to exposure, yet it is a necessary step.

If you cannot imagine a concrete desire, consider how you want the future to feel. There was a time for a number of years where I worked six days a week between my schoolwork, an internship, my day job, and later a full-time job with a part-time private practice. What kept me going was sensing that one day I could be in charge of my own employment. I did not know how that would look, but I could feel the lightness, the spaciousness, the joy of it. At times I found this feeling of the future more inspiring and sustaining than any affirmation or dream of success. When I experienced hardship with no goal, it was suffering. Knowing that goal meant I could use the hardship to water the seeds of that sensation. When I was at a crossroads, I could sense into which of my available options would lead to more of that feeling. After finishing graduate school and applying for jobs, I found an opportunity working with a population I would never have chosen for myself. Yet the person who would have been my supervisor radiated that sensation I wanted to have in my work—alive, curious, reflective, and engaged. When the job offer came, however, it was for a location much further away that would require driving through more city traffic and not working with that supervisor—more stress, less support, less spaciousness than the feeling I sought. Though parts of me screamed I should take whatever I could get, I decided to decline the offer. Within two days, I got a call back for the same position but now at the location I wanted and working under that supervisor. Sometimes risks pay off. Doing magic helps.

Envisioning the Best Possible Future

One magical tool for letting a better future guide our present is a time travel trance where we talk to a version of ourself living in the most desirable future. I offer this to therapy clients in their early twenties who feel overwhelmed by either having so many or so few options for their future, and terrified of making the wrong choice or remaining stuck. Though this trance rarely gives definitive answers about what to do next, it does tend to validate the work we're doing today and inspires hope for the future. We may fear the judgment or shame of our future selves, but they tend to have a great deal of understanding and appreciation for us. They've been there—they know we'll figure it out! And they know we need permission to take responsibility for the life in front of us, with a lot of enthusiastic support. They know we can get through hard times and come into joy and our own form of success.

EXERCISE

Trance to Visit Your Future Self

You may choose to record this trance or ask a friend to guide you through it. The instructions are simple enough that you could read through and go on your own journey, but having a recording or person to hold the container allows parts of you to relax and go more deeply into the experience. As always, make sure you are in a comfortable and safe space. Ideally, do this when you are well-rested, fed, and in moderately good spirits. If you are rarely in good spirits, aim for a time when you're willing to do an experiment.

Close your eyes or soften your gaze, and imagine a hall of many doors. Invite in the knowing that behind each of these doors is a version of your future. Let yourself imagine walking this hallway for a bit, taking in how it appears to you today. What do the doors look like? How does it feel to walk along this hall? Keep walking and seek the door that leads to your best possible future. You don't have to know what that best future is, only that there is a door leading to it. Your intuition will help you find it. If you find yourself in a terrifying or painful future, know that you can leave and find a better one.

Once you find the door, open it and step through. Take time to acclimate to this future. Are there scents? Is there a vision of where you are? How does it feel in your body to be in this future? There is a person moving around in this place. Take time to find them and notice them. This is the you who is of this best possible future. See what you notice about them. How old do they seem to be? How do they move through the space? What are they doing? How do you feel toward them? There are times when people can see their future self but things about the future are blanked out or hard to grasp. Do not worry about this. Parts of you may not be ready to take in all the information available. Focus on what you can perceive.

Get the attention of your future self, and see how they greet you. Let them know who you are. Ask them what they'd like to tell you about them and their life. Ask what advice they have for you. Stay with this, following the interaction that feels right. When you feel the conversation is complete, thank your future self and go back through the door. Close it behind you and let yourself come out of the hallway and back into your body. Take time to record what you've learned or experienced. Move to the next practice when you feel ready.

EXERCISE

Anchoring the Wisdom of Your Future Self

Call back to yourself the wisdom that your future self offered to you in the trance—words, visions, or a deep-felt sense of what it was like to be in their presence. The qualities of that self lie within you in this exact moment. Imagine where those qualities lie in your physical and energetic bodies. Sense them as seeds of potential, or notice if they have begun to sprout, flower, or fruit. Ask those qualities what magical support they need from you to continue to develop. They may have a specific practice they request. If not, consider the following options and see if any feels right: You could imbue a seed with the energy of these qualities and plant it in new potting soil that you can water and tend. Alternatively, you might find a stone or crystal that resonates with the qualities and breathe a portion of the energy of your future self into it so that you can hold it in times when you need an anchor. You could draw a picture of your future self expressing those qualities, breathe a portion of its energy into it, and then place it somewhere you can see it. You might also find a bottle or jar and fill it with objects expressing the qualities of that future self—herbs, symbols, oils, or other objects that speak to you about who you'd like to be. Once the bottle is full, breathe the energy of your future self into it, close it with a cap or cork, and place it on your altar. If you find this work useful, you may return to it whenever you like. Your future self could be a good friend and mentor.

Chapter 5

Time as Cycle

Cyclical time is the process of eternity, a constant fluctuation within an unchanging pattern. In a cycle, we could say there is no beginning or ending. There are also numerous beginnings that terminate what came before and endings that initiate the next arc of movement. The cycle is a fundamental rhythm. Its forward momentum carries us through familiar stations, places we've been before over and over. Each day seems to have its own characteristics no matter when they occur. Fridays tend to be days of joy, excitement, and relief at the approaching weekend. Mondays tend to be colored with the sober grumpiness of coming back after a break. Even those who work irregular shifts that don't correspond to the conventional work week use this language to make their experience understandable to others, like when a retail worker says "Today is my Friday" though it is Tuesday. These workers are compelled to work on the weekends so others get to enjoy those weekends as weekends. This is one way we try to force the cycle to act like a line. Our technologies allow us to disrupt our relationship with natural cycles, to stay up all night working or partying instead of sleeping when the sun is gone; and then to pummel our nervous systems with stimulants to keep ourselves awake when we need to work. Sleep, however, remains a basic necessity, and disrupting its cycle is bad for your health. People who go too long without sleep can become psychotic.

Cyclical time is a critical orientation for magical practitioners. We move from sunrise, to noon, to sunset, to midnight, to sunrise. Looking to the cycles of sun, moon, and season inform our approaches to magic. It is the weather report that helps us align to the prevailing currents of the moment. As we would not throw an outdoor pool party in December if we lived in Minnesota, knowing the cycles of time helps us plan wisely in our magic.

The Fourfold Energetic Movement

The foundational energies of Western magic are fourfold, and symbolized with all manner of fourfold patterns. In contemplating how to deepen our relationship with these cycles, let us look at the basics. The names I offer here help us make sense of the movement of the energy cycle, but as we experience them, we can rarely know the exact moment when one phase becomes the next. One phase waxes while the other wanes, so we feel an overlap in their energies. Readers familiar with common magical associations of elements will notice a variation in the elements associated with certain directions. Using the elements associated with the cardinal signs of the zodiac feels more aligned with the energetic cycle of spellwork.

> **Seed:** The seed emerges from the resolution of the last cycle and contains the wisdom of its ancestors and the potential of its descendants. In this phase, it is dormant. It lies inert, cold, silent, and still. In this, the seed embodies both death and the potential for life. This energy is associated with the north, midnight, and the dark moon. The seed expresses the earthy qualities of Capricorn in evoking both the fallow times of the winter season and an enormous capacity for ambition and growth.
>
> **Sprout:** Once the seed is planted in the conditions necessary to stir its life—a certain combination of soil, water, light,

and warmth—it becomes the sprout. The sprout unfurls with vigor and urgency, tenderness and surprising power as it breaks through seed walls and the layers of dirt between itself and the sun. The sprout wants to get things going and break through what does not serve. This energy is associated with the east, morning, and the waxing moon. The sprout expresses the fiery, springtime qualities of Aries, both impetuous and vulnerable as it emerges into the world.

Flower: As the sprout matures, it opens its beautiful flowers to the sun to take in vitality and fertilization. As the flower, it is strong, powerful, and steady, though active in sustaining its vitality and doing the work of taking in what it needs to manifest its potential in the next phase. This energy is associated with the south, noon, and the full moon. The flower expresses the watery, fertile qualities of Cancer in high summer, opening to receive and closing to protect.

Fruit: The fertile flower becomes fruit, both a tasty manifestation of itself and a source of seeds that will continue the cycle. This is the phase of full manifestation along with release and death as the fruit drops and begins to decay or is otherwise consumed. This energy is associated with the west, twilight, and the waning moon. The fruit expresses the airy qualities of Libra in autumn, when we must discern the best uses and distribution of our harvest. The association with air also evokes the ethylene gas that causes fruit to ripen, becoming more delicious and, eventually, decay.

Look to the associations with the four phases and pick one that will help you befriend these energies—the seasons, the directions, or the movements of the sun or moon. Notice, for example, where the moon is every day, and how you feel in relation to the moon.

Notice how the waxing moon feels different from the waning moon. Pay attention for one complete cycle, though I would recommend at least three cycles so you can feel the similarities as the phases recur. Then move on to the sun, or the seasons. As you experience consciously these different cycles, you build your inner vocabulary to feel the resonant similarities between the rising sun, the waxing moon, and spring. Then when you are in the stream of magic, you can discern their unique currents and bring them to your work.

One of the virtues of paying attention in this way is that it gives more options and complexity for magic. In early training, it is useful to take on the discipline of aligning your working with the magical energies of the moment—if you want more money, for example, wait until the new or waxing moon to work with its qualities of growth and increase. Working with the rhythms of nature helps slow down our magic, bringing us into alignment with the greater currents and encouraging patience in our practice. If you practice long enough, however, you may decide you want the money as soon as possible, conditions be damned—and that's when magic gets interesting. A few years ago when I was early into self-employment and still not making enough income to sustain myself, I felt an urgent need to get it moving and draw in clients. It was an unusually snowy day in Seattle and the roads were unplowed, but I went out for a walk to the nearby apothecary where I'd go for inspiration. After grabbing an incense blend for wealth, I went back home and saw it was a waning moon and not an indicated time for money magic. But I decided, screw it, I'd work with the tide. So instead of crafting my work to draw in wealth, I used the waning energies by chanting for the removal of obstacles that impeded the flow of wealth into my life.

There are so many ways to play within these cycles, and the twins are of help here. If you need to purge but the prevailing energy is to sprout, consider what you'd like to invite in to over-grow it. If you want to flower but the energy is fruiting and rotting, what would you like to remove that could open the way for what you want? If you're stuck on your intention, could you work on the cycles within the cycles to anchor what you need? A rising sun on a waning moon in the summertime offers all the powers of sprouting, fruiting, and flowering to varying degrees. With that moment, you could invite in the self-awareness you need to disperse the fears that keep you from claiming your full powers as a magic worker.

EXERCISE
Adjusting to Your Conditions

Consider how you could adjust your intention or your magical approach in the following situations:

- It's the dead of winter, under a full moon, after mid-night and you're tired of being lonely. You want a sexual or romantic partner yesterday, and you're going to do a spell right now.

- In late fall with a waning moon, you have bills piling up and want to draw in a windfall of money so that you can travel this winter.

- In the early spring at high noon, you get a text message from an ex-partner who's caused you mostly suffering, and it's time to cut the cords.

- Consider a desire you have for yourself right now, and make note of the current conditions: season, time of day, point in the lunar cycle. If you were to do a magical working right now for this desire, what would optimize your success?

The Grand Thematic Cycles

The cycles of the planets and signs in astrology offer a particularly useful map to align your work with the prevailing currents of energy, or to adapt as needed. The astrological chart is itself a cycle upon which are placed the positions of the planets, luminaries, and asteroids relative to us at the center. As astrology is an ancient system, your working could be simple or incredibly complex; if you find this introduction intriguing, you may pursue further study. Working with the planets has helped inspire my magic and think ahead into the future, which I normally do not enjoy. When doing slow magic, anchor to these cycles for information, inspiration, and structure. Even if you have no interest in astrology, it is interesting to note that those who practice magic deeply and attune to the outer world through the kind of contemplation practiced in the last section end up arriving at the same insights as those who do work with astrology. Working with any divinatory system will help you align. You might find if you check the astrology later that the planets happened to be in support of your intention.

The seven classical planets are the foundation of astrological timing, the "wandering stars" of the zodiac that we would now categorize as five planets and two luminaries, our sun and moon. Each of the planets has an associated day of the week in which its energies are particularly foregrounded, and a unique amount of time it takes to complete one circuit of the zodiac. Aside from the two luminaries, each has phases in which they appear to move backward from our vantage point, in retrograde. Of course, the planets themselves are not moving backward, but the horoscope centers our subjective position and tracks the location of the planets relative to where we stand. It's as though Jupiter is racing ahead of us in his work but then realizes he's left us behind and missed something important in the process, so he goes back to review and rework what's been done. Everything is moving as it is supposed to move, though we may feel jostled and unsettled. When reading the following associations with each planet, keep in mind that its symbolic involvement in issues is what we'd experience as both positive and negative. If Mars expresses the qualities of courage, will, and strength, it also includes experiences of aggression, cowardice, and powerlessness. When I begin a round of work with planetary energy, I expect to encounter obstacles and wounds related to it before I start to access its powers. On lucky days, there's the initial rush of experiencing your potential before you have to deal with everything that gets in the way of realizing it.

> **The Cycle of Safety and Nurturance:** The moon is the swiftest moving luminary, taking twenty-eight days to complete a full cycle around the horoscope. Its day of the week is Monday. The moon is involved with our basic needs and wounds around our bodies including safety, being nurtured, and where we find comfort. If you were born at night, the moon is the luminary with the greatest influence and guidance in your life. Silver or purple are colors related to the moon.

> **The Cycle of Purpose:** The sun takes 365ish days to complete a full cycle. Its day of the week is Sunday. The sun makes us feel the most alive, the most ourselves, and shows what encourages us to grow and take risks. If you were born during the day, the sun is the luminary with the greatest influence and guidance in your life. Yellow or gold are colors related to the sun.

> **The Cycle of Knowledge and Communication:** Mercury's cycle is so close to the sun that it also takes about 365

days to complete, but it infamously experiences three or four retrograde periods during the year, so the exact timing of a return can vary. Its day of the week is Wednesday. Mercury is involved both with how we mentally grasp and communicate our understanding of the world as well as how we participate in social interactions with others. In a way, it encompasses all the ways we exchange knowledge, goods, and services: communication, deceit, transportation, commerce, thievery. Mercury is also a planet governing the magical process itself, so it is worth acknowledging and checking its status even if you are not doing mercurial work. Orange is Mercury's color.

The Cycle of Value and Pleasure: Venus could be said to have two cycles, given that it both moves through the zodiac and pendulums between rising before the sun as the morning star or setting after the sun as the evening star. It takes about a year, give or take, to cycle the zodiac, but it follows a larger cycle of five years to return to exactly where it was, both in the sky and relative to the sun. Its day of the week is Friday. Venus is involved with what we value and how we are valued, including how we draw love and resources toward ourselves or repel what is unwanted. Thus Venus encompasses beauty and love as well as money. Green or pink are Venus's colors.

The Cycle of Vitality and Strength: Mars's cycle is between one and a half to two years to return to a particular degree in the zodiac, so it may be worth looking up timing if working with the planet. Its day of the week is Tuesday. Mars is involved with how we engage in conflict and assert ourselves, how we project our energy into the world. Mars is helpful with issues of will, power, and setting clear boundaries with others. Red is the color of Mars, associated with blood and iron.

The Cycle of Abundance and Luck: Jupiter's cycle is the next furthest, as the planet takes about twelve years to complete a full cycle. Its day of the week is Thursday. Jupiter is involved with our comprehension and experience of greater benevolent forces in life such as luck, leadership, kindly spirits, philosophy, and generosity. With Jupiter, we experience a world in which we are supported and beloved beyond our comprehension and things work out for the best. Blue is Jupiter's color.

The Cycle of Adversity and Discipline: Saturn's cycle takes approximately twenty-nine and a half years. Its day of the week is Saturday. Saturn is involved with our comprehension and experience of life's harder, non-negotiable challenges such as illness, harsh spirits, aging, death, and struggle. With Saturn, we experience a world in which success is not guaranteed, so we must learn how to take responsibility for ourselves and apply discipline toward what matters. Saturn is a harsh energy but a powerful teacher whose medicine is potent but bitter. Slow magic is Saturn's domain. Black is Saturn's color.

When you look to these cycles, you will likely be drawn to one or two more than the others. It's useful to notice which cycles feel like home, which cycles feel like horror, and which cycles seem completely irrelevant. Regardless of how we feel, all of these cycles coexist and influence us. Each offers unique challenges and powers, and may serve us at times in life. These great beings may teach us the humility of fate, or empower us to engage our destinies with magic. I find virtue in both, unsurprisingly, though there are times I emphasize one over the other.

In modern astrology, we also know there are other planets, asteroids, and dwarf planets with much longer orbits. As their cycles are so long, it is unlikely that you would focus on them for personal magic, but you might attend to them in collective work—groups, organizations, and nations. In *Cosmos and Psyche*, author Richard Tarnas provides an extensive analysis of astrological transits in the outer planets that predicted certain recurrent global themes, and his readings of the planets guides the following descriptions.[13] Uranus's cycle is approximately 84 years long and is involved with disruptive and revolutionary changes in consciousness and material reality through new discoveries or applications of technology, philosophy, or other ideas that change the world. Neptune's cycle is 164 years long and is involved with spiritual revelations and illusions, the dreamworld, the spiritual otherworlds, dissociation from our material existence, and connection to the essential oneness of all beings. Pluto's cycle is 248 years long and is involved with the deep unconscious and the structure of the psyche, as well as what gets repressed for the sake of civil society yet still rules us from below, such as taboo or criminal elements of the personality and society.

According to Tarnas, these outer planets, along with Jupiter and Saturn, trace the larger cycles of history and culture in ways both predictable and surprising. He showed, for example, how the conjunction of Saturn and Pluto tends to correspond to themes of epidemics, incarceration, the hardening of borders, and a rising trend toward authoritarianism, all of which have followed the most

---

13. Richard Tarnas, *Cosmos and Psyche: Intimations of a New World View* (Plume, 2006), 91–100.

recent Saturn-Pluto conjunction in January of 2020.[14] The last Saturn-Pluto conjunction in the early 1980s similarly coincided with the onset of the AIDS crisis, the so-called war on drugs, and escalating tensions between world powers that led to the fracturing of the Soviet Union into smaller independent states. Observing the consequences of this most recent Saturn-Pluto episode as an adult, I noticed intriguing sub-movements in the past four years—when Jupiter entered Pisces in 2021, it brought a surge of naive hope and joyful release when access to the COVID-19 vaccine was broad enough in the United States that those of us still living under great restriction felt safe enough to return to life. There was so much relief in reconnecting with others and the return of a sense of future. Then Jupiter went retrograde back into Aquarius for several months, coinciding with collective clarity that the vaccines weren't ending the pandemic and more infectious variants were on the rise, driving a return to restrictions.

Do the planets "cause" these things to occur? Are they the hands of a great cosmic clock that show us the unfolding of fate? Are they convenient bodies upon which to project our hallucinations of patterns upon? These are interesting questions, but what has been more useful to me is the grounding reminder that though cycles recur, change is ongoing. When we enter a period of history that feels particularly impossible to resist, terrifying, and horrible, we can also trust that its time will pass. The challenge is to survive until it passes. The opportunity, far more challenging, is to work with the energy of the difficult times to strengthen will and magic.

Contemplating and Activating

In approaching the planets and luminaries as teachers, we engage in contemplative presence with their energies and reflective practice.

---

14. Tarnas, *Cosmos and Psyche*, 209–56.

To contemplate, commit to attending to one of these planets or cycles for a span of time. Every day at a particular time, remind yourself of your intention by praying for the planet's aid and wisdom—look into the planetary hours of each day, and time your petition to the time of the planet's rulership.[15] Put an image that connects you to the qualities of the planet upon your altar and meditate upon it. I also have appreciated taking time to learn what we know about the physical planet from a scientific perspective. Throughout the day, commit to noticing when themes related to the planet's themes or energy comes to attention. If working with Venus, for example, contemplate what comes up in relationship to value, beauty, ugliness.

To reflect, look to where the planet is currently located in the sky and think back to previous moments in the cycle when it was there.[16] If you are tracking Jupiter, for example, explore the issues of the particular sign where it's located, then think of both what's happening in your life today and what happened twelve years ago that relates to these themes. My natal Jupiter is in Scorpio in my tenth house, presaging a fascination with secrets and the occult as part of my social identity. During my second Jupiter return—when it crosses the degree it was located in at my birth—I took a class with a local Pagan community to learn about the Iron Pentacle that propelled me into pursuing deeper study and practice. My third Jupiter return featured the publication of a book I'd written about the Iron Pentacle. The resonances of these histories feel eerie, especially when we don't work with them on purpose, so to speak.

---

15. There are websites and apps that offer easy breakdowns of the planetary hours, like the Planetary Hours Calculator at planetaryhours.net.

16. Resources I like for looking up planetary locations include Astrodienst's website (astro .com), the iPhemeris app (iphemeris.com), and occasionally a simple search engine search of "When was the last time *planet* was in *sign*?"

EXERCISE
Befriending the Planets

Pick a planetary energy and a cycle to track its movements in your life. It's useful to journal about this in a way that works for you. Tune in to the planet on its particular day of the week to feel how its energies are present in you. If you have a relationship with a spirit or deity whose concerns are related to the planet, take time to make offerings or prayers on this day.

Consult an astrological chart or service to see where in the zodiac the planet currently is, and research the themes and issues of the sign it is currently inhabiting. Look at previous times in your life that the planet inhabited this sign or degree—what was happening then? What were you struggling with or learning? How does that relate to what is present in your life today? Research the next time this planet will be in this sign. Where would you like to be when these issues become active in your life again?

Illustrate this with a picture or a short paragraph, and then burn it in a safe place until it becomes ash. Take a candle in a color related to the planet you're working with—if you can't find one, white is fine—and rub it with the ashes of your intention while petitioning the planet or related spirits for aid. On a day related to the planet, burn the candle completely. If you reach the end of the day and have more candle left, snuff out the flame and wait until the next week when the planetary day comes around again.

Practical Applications

Engaging the planets and luminaries magically engages them as partners, mentors, and co-conspirators. As you align your magic with the qualities most supportive of its achievement, so in turn do the planetary energies shape you and your magic. To empower yourself against those who take advantage and ignore your voice, you could call in the powers of Mars by charging your working on a Tuesday and wearing the color red, burning dragon's blood or cinnamon incense. To engage in deep, profound integration of this transformation, you could commit to honoring and empowering yourself with Mars every Tuesday for a full martial cycle. But if you're averse to warrior energy, you could try the approaches of Venus or Jupiter to elevate your worth in their eyes.

Here is an opportunity to add more complexity, joining the fourfold energetic cycle with astrological timings to support ambitious and long-term workings: the cycles of interaction between two or more heavenly bodies.[17] For this, we attend to times when two or more planets and luminaries conjoin—that is, appear to be in the same degree on the horoscope. In the conjunction, the planets blend their essences to become a unique composite being bearing all the conflicts and potentials of its member planets. If it's a useful blending, we'll want to turn our sails to catch that wind and let it propel us forward on a cycle that continues until the next conjunction of these beings. The swiftest-moving planet of the conjunction will be the one whose journey we follow as it moves across the circuit of the zodiac. It is as though the conjunction of the planets look together at a great question, and then the swifter planet is tasked with working that question thoroughly according to its nature. From the seed of that conjunction, the swifter planet expresses the energy of the cycle, sprouting until it flowers in opposition with the slower planet, then coming to fruition as it returns to the conjunction in a different sign from the last, as the

---

17. The following process of tracing conjunctions is adapted from Dane Rudhyar and
    Leyla Rael, *Astrological Aspects: A Process-Oriented Approach* (Red Wheel/Weiser, 1980),
    31–33.

slower planet has moved on, ready to seed the question anew from a different perspective.

This timing strategy is implicit in the witchcraft practice of aligning workings with the cycle of the moon. As the swiftest-moving luminary who lives closest to us, the moon is uniquely suited to take in the energies of the heavens and bring them into manifestation on earth. When the moon is new, it conjoins the sun, bringing the seeds it has gathered from its previous cycle. The sun inspires the seeds with brilliant visions of solar purpose, but those visions are too distant to survive the material plane. As the moon waxes, those visions sprout and gain foothold in our lives, tempered and cooled by the necessities and limitations of life on this planet. When the moon is full, it opposes the sun. The flowering of that inspiration is open to earth's fertile power, creating the fruit that we harvest as the moon wanes. We may be disappointed with the manifestation; it is rarely as wondrous as the vision. Yet without the vision, it would not be. As the moon returns to its dark phase, conjoining the sun, it offers the seeds of those fruits for new inspiration.

EXERCISE
Deeper Study of Planetary Cycles

Look back to the luminaries and planets and their themes to see if there are two that particularly speak to you. Look up how frequently these bodies conjoin each other and when the last conjunction occurred. Usually a simple search on your preferred internet search engine will get you what you need, but you could also consult a digital or physical ephemeris. Consider what was happening in the world at large and for you in your personal life during these conjunctions.

Chapter 6

TIME AS SPIRAL

Orbiting a galactic center, our sun moves along its own gravitational arc, leading its system of planets and asteroids that followed in their own orbits. Cycles within cycles moving along a path reveal that the solar system is a spiral, corkscrewing through time and space.[18] A spiral integrates both the forward trajectory of the line and the recurrence of the cycle to emerge as the peacock of these twins. While we are fated to keep reexperiencing certain themes and struggles, we do so informed by all we have learned in our previous circuits. We have more spaciousness, a new perspective, or new circumstances. We can never go back, though we may look to what came before for inspiration. This perspective is both humbling and immensely relieving when it comes to living.

Like many, I still get frustrated or discouraged when old issues resurface—"Didn't I deal with this?" If I only believed in the line, I would see this as a sign of having moved backward in my progress. Then I'd beat myself up, and my impatience might get in the way of what I could learn from the moment. If I only believed in the cycle, I would be resigned to the resurgence with an "of course" and wait it out until it inevitably passes and better times come. Then I'd languish and not push myself to continue learning

---

18. mujobrod, "Real Movement of Sun and Planets: Solar system as vortex," April 17, 2022, https://www.youtube.com/watch?v=GMFw-8zlgv0.

or growing, forgetting that I participate. With the spiral, though resurgence is expected, we have options. When we experience moments of contraction and illness, we meet them with conscious awareness and the effort to keep exercising ourselves so that we lose less ground. When we experience moments of joy and abundance, we meet those with the conscious awareness to savor and enjoy these moments while preparing for them to pass.

Often, folks talk about spiraling as a destructive movement. The common image is of a downward spiral into destructive behavior and despair: shame spirals, anxiety spirals, depression spirals. The spiral of a plane whose engine has failed but is still coasting along the currents of air, down to its doom. In this form of the spiral, failure and pain confirms a horrible belief about ourselves that leads to more suffering, more accidents and failures, more confirmation of our worst stories. Fear of such spirals makes us more cautious about taking risks and making changes in life. Impatience to correct the spiral leads people to set themselves up to fail with unrealistic goals or to try multiple solutions but give up before any can take effect. Both approaches make further downward spirals more likely because they do not help us feel the competency and self-esteem we need.

There is an upward spiral. Once I was in a beautiful place in the desert, gazing at the mountains, and saw a hawk spiraling up high into the sky. It had caught a warm updraft and broke its forward soaring to begin to circle, letting the air carry it as high as it wanted to go. Slow magic is the art of cultivating this spiral. The virtue of this approach is gentleness with ourselves, using what we've learned from the cycle to bolster our work. In this spiral, we set achievable goals, succeed in working on them, experience success, and justify empowering beliefs about ourselves, giving us confidence to take the next risk. With every turn of this spiral, there is more space and perspective rooted in the evidence of our capability. That confidence is hard to destroy.

Crafting Your Upward Spiral

Say that you know getting more movement would be good for your body and your mood, and going for daily walks would help. But it's wintertime, and you hate being cold! You could work with these time conditions to boost your intention to overcome your aversion to the cold and push yourself to start your walks—doing spellwork with the powers of east and air, or dedicating your energy by committing to do your walks at dawn. (If this works for you, may you be blessed. It is not my path.) On the other hand, you might accept that you're not likely to walk while it's cold, but you could look into indoor movement options that are achievable and would honor your intention while you wait for the weather to turn. The teaching is, as you might be noticing, to honor the polarities and contradictions and let them help you find your way to engage your will regardless of what is happening. If you know you would benefit from movement now, it is worthwhile to find a way you can begin actively doing it today. Saying, "Never mind, I'll wait a few months" is as detrimental as being too ambitious and failing.

EXERCISE
Moving from Struggle to Upward Spiral

Identify a place in your life where you feel you are struggling or failing—in a discipline, at work, at home, in relationships with others or yourself. Try to set aside time where you can be uninterrupted and calm in doing this work, perhaps lighting a candle or creating sacred space to support you. You may want to contain this work by doing each reflective practice for a half hour at a time, with a day or so of break in between.

Start with the twin of linear time: What is the story of this struggle? When did it begin? What are key events that have happened up until now regarding this struggle, positive or negative? What do you see as the future you are living into with this struggle? What signs tell you this struggle is getting better or worse?

When you are ready, move to the twin of cyclical time: Looking at the previous narrative, do you see any patterns? Could you map those out into a cycle that tends to recur? For example: "I talk to my boss about being over-whelmed and underpaid. She promises I will be getting a raise soon and that she'll try to lighten my burden. Work feels easier for a while. My boss gives me an additional project that demands I work overtime. I get less sleep and feel depressed."

When you are ready, engage with the peacock of spiral time: Reflect or journal about the following questions, setting aside questions of practicality or potential consequences for the moment: What future would you desire to live into instead of the one you wrote for linear time? If you could interrupt this cycle to push it toward a direction of your desire, where would you intervene? What change could you make to feel more success in this cycle? What resources or supports would empower you to make and sustain this change?

Once you have answers, take some time to let them sit in you before coming back with your concerns and fears about making these changes. Name at least one way you can interrupt this cycle that is achievable and within your power, no matter how small. Craft a piece of spell-work to support you in making this change. Remember that according to the model of spiral time, you may make this change and still go through a version of the cycle, but pay attention to whether this round feels easier and freer or heavier and more constrictive. Let that information inform you for your next effort in interrupting the cycle.

Magic Across Time

Accepting the reality of the spiral means preparing for every turn of the screw, knowing that we will have setbacks when life is going well, and remembering there will be joy when life is difficult. We come into the world with the innate potentials and challenges of our horoscope depicting the relationship of the planets at the moment of our birth. Everyone alive experienced that horoscope when you were born, but for most it was a brief episode of their story. For you, it is the thematic core. You embody it. Wherever you go in life, you carry within you the gifts and struggles of the season and conditions of your birth, though you can go deeply into exploring and refining them. Spellwork is much the same in that it crystallizes the power of a moment of time so that it is always available when you need it or it activates a future possibility in the now. When I feel strong joy or peace, I pause to send a breath of that energy back in time to my younger self when he was struggling and didn't understand why.

EXERCISE
Capturing the Past for Future Need

The next time you have a day where you feel particularly joyful, happy, safe, or any lovely feeling that you'd like to have in your life—get a bowl and fill it with water. That night, leave it in a place where the light of the moon and stars can touch it. This may be challenging, but make your best effort. Before the sun touches it in the morning, bring the bowl inside and put the water in a spray bottle or any other container you can keep for a long time. Whenever life feels hard and you feel distant from that lovely feeling, mist yourself with the moon water of that day or use it for another kind of work. (I do not recommend drinking it unless you filter or boil it first!)

Long-Range Visioning

Slow magic is a collaborative process. We both create and perceive the future, particularly when we study the currents of the river to see how they're flowing. Some folks distinguish intuition that comes from paying close attention and seeing patterns from "real" psychic awareness that receives information through another process, but this distinction has never made sense to me. Divination comes when we pay attention with presence, softness, and openness, both observing what is in front of us and receiving subtle cues. But it is also like a game—our attention is held within limitations and rules that seem arbitrary but necessary. Whether you lay three tarot cards or twenty, whether you watch the clouds or the stock exchange, the process of attention allows you to focus on the patterns while other senses expand to receive other kinds of information. I met an accountant who could look at a client's finances and tell exactly what was happening and what was to come in their lives. After years of study and practice, the numbers told him a story with as much predictive power as a tarot spread.

Seeing into the future, then, is a skill one can cultivate. Yet the further ahead we try to look, the more murky and foggy that perception becomes. Trying to perceive the future feels like standing on the bow of a ship trying to discern the contents of a coastline from a great distance. When it's too far away, it's hard to see with accuracy. You may be able to see vague shapes that become clearer as you grow closer. If you're tempted to guess what those vague shapes are, you may get lucky or you may be wrong. Looking back, one can see scientific, political, and artistic divinations about the crises of 2020. Various scientists, epidemiologists, and researchers anticipated the rise of a global pandemic years before COVID-19 came to our doors. There were also so many movies with characters living through a horrible catastrophe that occurred in the world that could only be avoided by staying inside. Whether it was zombies, monsters with incredible hearing, flesh-eating mist, or actual illness, there was a looming horror of the expansive world and a sense of being both safe and trapped within the confines of home—encapsulating the emotional experience of the COVID years, though not the literal truth.

Long-term divining work helps us to know the currents we'll be navigating as we traverse the twins. In the years leading up to 2016, numerous spirits and gods warned those who would listen of a storm that was coming and to build their resilience.[19] The events following 2016 felt like a storm of increasing strength and destruction with occasional surges and easing of intensity. Perhaps we were living through the prophecy—not because of one politician, but because the conditions of the climate made a storm inevitable. That is a linear view. From the cyclical perspective of a storm god, there is always a storm coming, a storm occurring, and a storm passing away. In the United States, we found ourselves in stormy times

---

19. John Beckett speaks to this history in his column, particularly "The Storm is Strengthening–Put Your Faith in Deeper Things," *Under the Ancient Oaks* (blog), April 24, 2018, https://www.patheos.com/blogs/johnbeckett/2018/04/the-storm-is-strengthening-put-your-faith-in-deeper-things.html.

after decades of relative prosperity and peace at the expense of other nations enduring their own storms. From a distance, we experience these great cycles as fate. At close range—where we live—we are in the chaos, and chaos is rich with possibilities. We have the choice and freedom to reject or resist our divinations or to change the plan and thus our destiny, requiring a new divination.

The Annual Divination

I have done this practice annually since 2012, when I approached my last year of graduate school. I needed to complete an internship and start thinking about my postgraduate career. Knowing I would avoid dealing with any of this without structure, I used tarot to seek guidance on how best to use my time in moving toward these goals, and accountability to keep me in action. Divining a month at a time, I received encouragement, challenges, and tasks to pursue. At times, the tasks did not seem to make sense. At other times, the tasks were exactly the things I knew were necessary that I'd otherwise avoid. Having these messages written down made them feel like a homework assignment, and I've always been one who feels like I have to complete my homework, so that helped me to follow through on uncomfortable tasks. If you don't like homework, pretend I didn't write that and see if there's a way this practice might be encouraging to you. Having this guidance from your reading is like having the encouragement and accountability of a coach or a monthly love note from an ardent admirer. Having done this work for more than a decade, I find that following the guidance and information sets me up for what's to come. By the time I open the envelope for the next month, what once made no sense now feels exactly right. I've already begun to sense what would be the next step, and the envelope's contents confirm it.

Doing this work has felt both challenging and comforting, like having a wise friend walking with me, keeping me focused on my spiritual work amidst the turmoil. Yet that wise friend happens to be my god soul, supported by the gods. I've had scary readings that turned out not to be so awful once they happened. I've had relatively mild-sounding readings for what turned out to be awful months when I needed gentle support. I feel the action of both destiny and fate, that while my god soul lays out the path, I choose to walk it, and divination confirms it. It's more fun than knowing exactly what the future will bring. This practice lets me stay connected to my intuition and spiritual practice, and it helps me feel bolstered by great hands and eyes that have my back. But then it lets me be curious. It lets me approach the world with wonder and no knowledge of what is coming. It lets me be surprised and excited. During 2020, having done my annual divination in Samhain of 2019, I had a number of sealed envelopes with guidance for the future written before news of the coronavirus caught any attention. Having felt no warning of a looming global crisis, I wondered if the cards would feel wholly irrelevant when I opened them. Yet the guidance continued to feel right—exactly what I needed, though I didn't "know" what was coming: guidance to work on processing grief and listening to intuition, and prompts to organize and offer workshops when I otherwise would have wanted to withdraw and wait out the stress.

We are about to look at my framework for doing an annual divination practice. As with all these workings, you can modify if you wish, using your preferred divination tools or dividing the year into segments that resonate with you. Many witches and magicians I know have a practice like this and may do this working for themselves and for the future of their covens or other organizations. If you have a deep relationship with a psychopomp or spirit of divination and prophecy, you may choose to work with them. My annual readings have been devotionals to Anubis, one who goes into the dark places, finds the paths, and protects those who seek. If you do not have relationship with a psychopomp, Anubis is friendly to those who approach with respect.

Connecting with Anubis

Take time to look up images, texts, and stories associated with Anubis. Try to look at a few different versions to get a sense of the range of this being and the ways he manifests to others. My experience is that Anubis tends to be a scout and may come to you as soon as he senses your interest. Pay attention to your dreams and trances and see if he shows up. For a more formal introduction, go out into nature where you'll be undisturbed. Either go to a physical location or bring yourself into trance and go into a wild place. As you walk toward this place of nature, physical or otherwise, see if you find any animal bones on the way; if you do, take one with you. Even in my urban neighborhood I am stunned by how many animal bones are around.

Find the place to connect and stop. Breathe. Connect to the place. Throw the bone to the ground. Repeat the following nine times: "Anubis, you, friend to the seekers and the lost, you who lighten the hearts and help us find the way. Please come to me." Wait. Listen. Notice. If you sense the presence of the god, tell him what you'd like help in seeking. You can be as vague or specific as you like. Listen for what he needs from you. When things feel complete, return home. Pay attention to your dreams that night.

Craft a Spirit Lamp

In the Greek Magical Papyri, there is a spell for divining that features the wick of the lamp associated with the mummification bandage that Anubis uses to wrap the body of Osiris.[20] Hurricane lamps tend to be pretty low cost and accessible, and they have thick wicks that look like bandages. To add more clarity and guidance to your divinations, acquire a lamp you will dedicate to this purpose. Cast a circle or create sacred space with the lamp present. Sprinkle blessed salt water over the lamp or wave the smoke of cleansing herbs across the lamp's surface. Say, "May you be cleansed and purified of your past uses. May you join with my purpose."

Call to the god with the words in your heart. You might say, "Great jackal, black dog, you who walk the between places and guard the lost and the seeking. As you are the one who carries light into the darkest places, so I offer you this lamp. When its flame burns, may it illuminate the gnosis you bring forth." Light the lamp and gaze upon it for several breaths. Breathe energy from below and above into your core, and send it into the lamp. Imagine the god pouring his own energy into the lamp until it glows or vibrates with divine power. Trace a pentacle over the lamp to seal the energies within it.

Divining for the Year

I do this divination around the time of Samhain. If you want to be precise, look for the date of when the sun is in 15 degrees of Scorpio. Now that I do this working with others, I prefer the astrological date, as it tends to be slightly past the busy witchy season of Halloween. You could also do this working on the secular new year's day or your own birthday. I like Samhain because it's said to be the witch's new year and a time when it is easier to pierce the veil between worlds to access gnosis and spirit contact.

---

20. Hans Dieter Betz, *The Greek Magical Papyri in Translation,* 2nd ed. (University of Chicago Press, 1992), 204.

Have available eight to twelve envelopes and pieces of paper, plus a pen. I buy stationary card sets that have matching envelopes and cards. The number of envelopes and cards depends on what markers of time you want to use for your reading. I do twelve because I work with the months of the zodiac, but others do eight and work with the solstices, equinoxes, and cross-quarter holidays. Also have your lamp ready (if you have one) and a sortilege divination tool from which you pull an object for each moment in time.

Breathe, center, and align your souls. Cast a circle. Call upon your preferred psychopomp to come to your aid. If you are working with Anubis, you are welcome to use this prayer:

> *Blessed are you, Black Dog,*
> *You who find the secret ways.*
> *Open our senses, lighten*
> *the burdens in our hearts*
> *that we may live in truth.*
> *In the shadow of this flame,*
> *gather Your gnosis for us,*
> *bringing gold from darkness*
> *so that we may know joy*
> *in the work to come.*

Shuffle your deck and draw a card for the upcoming month. Observe the card and notice what advice, information, or guidance comes through. Record this on one of your pieces of paper. When things feel complete, seal the paper in one of the envelopes, and write the month on the front of the envelope. Then draw a card for the following month. Do the same as before. Continue this process until you've read for each upcoming month and have sealed envelopes that will get you through to the next turning of the cycle. I use the zodiacal months for my readings, so I start my readings with Sagittarius and go through the year until I get to the next Scorpio season.

Thank the god for support and extinguish the flame. Close your circle. Put the envelopes on your altar. Wait until it is time to open each one. Occasionally, I'll get eager and open next month's a day or so early, but it's been lovely to have these cards waiting for me, holding knowledge I may or may not remember, as well as to experience the surprise and delight of seeing the divination again when the time has come to work with it.

If I wrote all the guidance together on a journal page, I would keep anxiously checking ahead and worrying about the future. With the envelopes, you can focus on what's right in front of you this month and know you'll be supported in the months to come. Knowing that future you will be thankful for the work you're doing today, and future you will be able to focus on their work when the time comes.

Planting Seeds

A friend of mine once took me to a widespread and influential group focused on personal development and taking intense responsibility for one's life. They placed a strong value on standing up and speaking your intentions for change in front of the group. If you told everyone what you wanted to do, then you'd do it. This practice seemed at odds with my witchcraft practice that values the power of silence in gathering power for manifestation.[21] Talking without discretion invites other people's suggestions, criticisms, and doubts, all of which may throw our own parts into confusion and conflict. Once you've set your intention and activated your

---

21. T. Thorn Coyle, *Make Magic of Your Life: Passion, Purpose, and the Power of Desire*, (Weiser, 2013), 147–63.

spell, fussing over it and talking about it too much is like constantly opening the microwave to check if it's heating your food. We need a tight, well-maintained container for the magic to do its work until it has reached the state you desire.

Psychological research offers a complementary insight to the approach of keeping silence. A group of neuroscientists published a study in 2009 asserting the theory that goal-directed activity is motivated by reflecting upon the desired goal and contrasting it with the obstacles to that goal in present reality.[22] While observing brain activity during this mental contrasting, they saw significantly higher neurological activation than when observing a subject "merely daydreaming" about the desired future. The neurological activation of mentally contrasting desire with present obstacles includes the prefrontal cortex, which as we have discussed relates to executive functioning and will. It is not enough to simply announce once's goals or daydream about a better future. We need to do the work of thinking about why in our current conditions we have not already realized our goals, and what needs to change.

There is value in having mentors and community to witness our goals and support us in accountability, but we need more selectivity than announcing it to whomever might listen. A more recent study suggests that we're more likely to finish what we started when we tell people we admire, whose approval we want.[23] Twelve-step programs get this right, allowing their participants to show up exactly as they are to be witnessed in community and held accountable to their commitments. Being fully witnessed by self

---

22. Anja Achtziger, Thorsten Fehr, Gabriele Oettingen, Peter M. Gollwitzer, and Brigitte Rockstroh, "Strategies of intention formation are reflected in continuous MEG activity," *Social Neuroscience* 4, no. 1 (2009): 11–27.

23. Howard J. Klein, Robert B. Lount, Hee Man Park, and Bryce J. Linford, "When goals are known: The effects of audience relative status on goal commitment and performance," *Journal of Applied Psychology* 105, no. 4 (2020): 372–89.

and others is potent, especially when they witness with full acceptance of who we are today and who we want to become. We start to move toward integrity. This requires the inner and outer safety to be as you are, the power of naming your desire, and the courage of looking at the gap between the two. In generative witnessing, god soul is present with its endless wellspring of love, nourishing the parts of us that used to work so hard. I want to rest and play and not always be a machine for making money or accruing status and social power. I want softness and power.

Witchcraft and certain threads of chaos magic offer a kind of magic that isn't about making announcements or holding one's self accountable. This magic roots in the animal soul, though it may start from the human soul in terms of intention. This kind of magic is about forgetting. Plant the intention into your deep unconscious and then discard it, let go of all investment in its coming to fruition. Live your life. Let the working grow deep beneath the ego's fervid, micro-managing gaze. In the dark, the spell has the power to take root and sprout on its own terms, guiding us from below. Studies of neurological activity suggests that the brain begins to make a decision up to ten seconds before we are consciously aware of the choice we're making.[24]

The gestation magic we are about to explore is the epitome of slow magic. Its process allows us to petition the masters of fate and our deep unconscious for profound change. We can use gestation magic for those desires that seem too big to imagine. Too unruly to master. Too overwhelming to know where to begin. To map a path, you must know at least two points: where you are, and where you want to be. Without these coordinates, there's nothing to chart. Yet plotting these points brings up so much resistance and avoidance.

24. Roger Koenig-Robert and Joel Pearson, "Decoding the contents and strength of imagery before volitional engagement," *Scientific Reports* 9 (2019): 3504.

When my goals are too big and scary, I tend to shut down. I become so anxious and overwhelmed by the not-knowing of how to do something that I end up avoiding the desire altogether. Or I set up a goal that's way too ambitious to succeed in the time I imagined, and fail, and get discouraged. Then there's nowhere to go and life feels cyclical or beset by randomness without much purpose. Gestation magic begins in this moment and uses time as a structure to help you think of where you want to go, much like the Rose of Desire in that we ask for the steps to come to us after we've launched our goal.

Gestation Magic

For this practice, I use an envelope and pieces of paper. You might opt to use a bottle or other sealable container. Decide whether you want to work for a month from now, year from now, or ten years from now—however long you dare to set your course. Write that future date on the front of the envelope. Think about what you want to have manifested in your life at that time. If there is a concrete and specific outcome, write that down. You might, however, write down any qualities that feel right: "Stable health," "no debts," "loving partnership," or any such phrase. You don't have to have any idea how you'll get there. What I like to do is tear a piece of paper into sections and write one of these qualities upon each scrap. Put whatever you've written in the envelope. If you want to draw pictures or print out images of things you want, go for it.

When things feel complete, spend a lot of time sitting with the unsealed envelope. Slow down your breathing. As you inhale, tense all your muscles, and then release them as you exhale. Get soft. Imagine the power of the earth easily and naturally rising into your body, gathering in your belly center. So, too, the powers of the sky easily and naturally sink through your head and heart into your belly. Breathe until these centers are radiant with power. Exhale while imagining this radiance pouring outward through your mouth into the envelope. Let that power and radiance saturate the envelope and all it contains. The power of earth and sky refill you between each exhale. When the envelope vibrates and shimmers with power, seal it shut and kiss the seal.

Let the envelope sit on your altar or a place where it won't be disturbed but you'll remember to open it when the time comes. Then, live your life and try not to think too much about what you put in the envelope. In the intervening time, if you feel called to do other kinds of magic, go for it. Trust that your intuition guides your instincts and unfolding inner process. When you've reached the target date, create a sacred space and open your envelope. Look through its contents. Reflect on the extent to which these desires are manifest in your life today and journal the outcomes. Dispose of the envelope and papers in a way that honors their service to you. But wait—the spell isn't over yet! In my experience, opening the envelope is the flowering phase. The working bears fruit the following weeks. Keep paying attention.

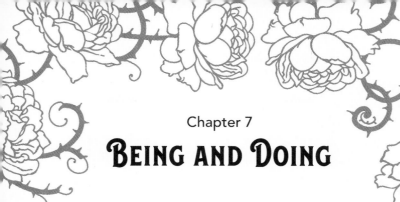

Chapter 7

BEING AND DOING

Slow magic invites us to look at our patterns of work and play, running energy and resting to recover over a long duration. We can get too task-y, physically going through the motions while mentally and spiritually being elsewhere. We can also be so in the moment and at our ease that we do not get around to the work at hand. Here the divine twins come forward again wearing new faces, revealing their relationship to magical energy. These twins express the polarities of how we engage in the matters of life, how comfortable we are with asserting ourselves, how much or how little we exert influence. They embody the qualities of activity and passivity, heat and coolness, assertiveness and receptivity. These twins bear several names and appear in widely recognized symbols, often ascribed to masculinity and femininity. Regardless of our own gender, we have access to their powers and vulnerabilities. Today I name them "Doing" and "Being."

Most of us know doing well: getting involved with the matters of life, taking action, taking initiative, and managing the outer world. Doing fills our days. In the culture of the United States, we define ourselves by what we do. As adults meeting new acquaintances, one of the first questions to ask is, "What do you do?" When not discussing what we do for work, we talk about what we did on weekends. We are all so busy with doing. We evaluate ourselves through the lens of productivity, even when it comes to emotional experiences. People bemoan grief or depression as unproductive, as though every life experience must work toward specific measurable outcomes to have value. This emphasis on accomplishment above all pervaded my high school and college experience, as I met competitive young millennials who'd completed impressive internships before I'd figured out how to get a normal job. Doing was what people valued the most.

Of course, doing is important. It is part of the deal of being an incarnate human with needs and desires, living in a society that expects participation. If we didn't do, we would have no books, no art, no crops, no technology, no roads, no aid or support for each other. At this point, I need to work for money to have access to the basic needs and joys of life—nourishing food, clean water, dry shelter, loving partnership, things like that. Those who aspire to opt out of dominant culture must do a lot to meet these needs. Doing all the time starts to make life narrow, gray, and lifeless. Doing is like swimming. It's a great option to get from one side of the river to the other. But if you never get to stop swimming—if you keep paddling and kicking and the shore never comes—it's exhausting. Anxiety and panic creep in as we worry that there's no ground to stand upon, no moment to breathe, no hope for rest or joy. We forget we could soften and let the current carry us or seek help.

Turning toward being from this incessant doing is an immense relief. Being offers an ever-renewing source of presence and compassion. We find in being that loving partner, that attentive parent, that compassionate god we've been seeking outside of ourselves. It offers companionship and support so that we are not alone. It tells us who we truly are and lets us know that we are okay at our most basic level. There is nothing to prove and nothing to fix. No conditions on who or what we are. Worries and anxieties, tensions and outrages begin to melt. Being does not solve external problems or ameliorate the injustices and oppressions of the world. It extends ease, acceptance, and contact with the ground and sky that gives us strength and breadth. Being is like floating. Instead of all that heavy effort and contortion, we relax and expand and let ourselves be buoyed and carried along by the current. It's calm. There's no agenda. We might be sitting taking in a good book, soaking up the sun, or walking in the woods.

Surrendering to being may be a struggle, especially when doing feels so important to our survival and success. Indeed, some of us need to make an effort to create the container that would allow us to be—setting clear boundaries to protect personal time, saving the money to go on a long vacation, or engaging in the discipline of sitting practice. After almost two decades of practicing sitting meditation, I still notice how worry, planning, and analysis clamor for attention, urgent about their concerns. I may spend minutes in a meditation posture but inwardly I am elsewhere, not being with myself. Sometimes if it's been too long since I've had a vacation, I'll experience the first couple days as a strange depressive letdown, like my soul is decompressing before I can experience the lift and fullness of being at ease. Being encompasses the vast multiplicity of truths and perspectives, giving our parts space to coexist in the vast field of silence that already exists within us. Trying to get involved with our thoughts and feelings to change them puts us back into doing and is like shaking a snow globe in the hopes that we'll get the flakes to settle.

Parts of us may try to get around this resistance to being by getting drunk or high, checking out, or numbing ourselves. These strategies can be intense, costly, and sometimes illegal. They can also seem more innocuous. Sometimes the things we do to relax or unwind end up becoming forms of checking out, like watching television or playing video games past the point where it's fun and into a state of numbness. It's like these parts of us are trying to shut down our over-active doers and get us into a state of ease while still hesitant to embrace being. When we stop and rest, feelings we've been avoiding have a tendency to catch up. Yet it is the capacity of being with these emotions that allows them to heal and move through us. If you find there are parts of you that compulsively engage in intoxicating, numbing, or checking-out behaviors, it is worth seeking out a therapist or community who can support you in understanding them, processing the feelings they're avoiding, and generating other ways for these parts to help you to feel alive.

An excess of being offers its own traps and forms of exhaustion. With too much floating, we lose where our bodies end and the river begins. This blurring matters because our bodies have needs that are not the river's concern. The world is as full of venom and sharp edges as it is nourishment and soft resting places. Floating through the rapids and being jostled against rocks by the river's current is scary, painful, and sometimes unnecessary. Tolerating hardship without cultivating safety and joy eventually lands us in cynicism and resentment. If we keep pushing away our anger and hurt—the parts of us trying to warn us that what we're doing isn't working—being becomes resignation and numbness. Eventually that rejected rage and hurt will erupt.

When I'm doing too much, I start to feel tense, anxious, empty, and robotic, and I struggle to rest or give up responsibilities. At worst, I'm a martyr. When I'm being too much, I slide into depression and despondency, at worst resisting any impulse to get up and do, feeling hopeless about the future. Neither of these extremes are necessary. The more we become acquainted with our tendencies, the better we are at sensing the subtle signs of when it's time to engage the other. Yet as with all the twins, we seem prone to making them war with each other, holding up one as good and the other terrible. To illustrate this war in action, here's a story.

One of the great magical workings I've undertaken in my adult life is the effort to manifest strong spiritual community. As a person who loved the Catholic church in my childhood but felt unable to continue to participate in it as an adult, I followed a dream of growing a new, wildly joyful and affirming Pagan community where all could be seen and accepted with open hearts and strong wills. Unfortunately, building community is a difficult process. Often I found myself in positions of leadership, sitting in conversations about policy and documentation to respond to community problems. I felt drained and impatient with these processes (which do matter) and guilty when I imagined not showing up for the work I hated in favor of focusing on what I loved—the ritual and practice.

My problem was twofold: a tendency to volunteer for too many things and doing them as quickly as possible. I'm a person who learned early in life to get his homework done before he could have any fun, and that mindset had me sitting on a conference call on a Sunday morning, agreeing to write a proposal for this and a description of that, and then spending the following hour after the call doing all that writing and emailing it to everyone so I could move on with my life, eating up more of my weekend in the process. Others, however, did not seem to have the same urgency. There's been many a call in which a number of us agreed to do a piece of work but a month later we'd get back on the call and I was one of the few who completed their task. I told myself a story that if I wanted things done, I would have to do it myself. This impatience became its own burden as I started to resent doing so much of the work, feeling like I was carrying groups with my own labor. Not doing the work made me feel guilty and terrified that everything would fall apart and I'd be blamed. Now I see how much my behavior created the situations I didn't want. Others have validated my sense that my efforts were appreciated and recognized, as well as taken for granted at times. My compulsive volunteering and doing might have intimidated, embarrassed, or annoyed others who had less urgency, more difficulty following through, or better boundaries. I did not have the patience to let others step up in their own time. Some might have been wholly capable of doing the work but needed more structure and accountability than I knew to provide. Some might have wanted more mentorship and support and not known how to ask for it. Some might have simply assumed that I liked doing all this work and saw no reason to interrupt it.

There was no doubt an unfairness in my expectations of others, reflecting how often I felt expected of more than was reasonable. Frequently I've taken on heavy responsibilities without mentorship and support. As a young adult, I was often teased for not knowing basic life skills that no one had taken the time to teach me. I've been made a teacher or a leader without training or oversight. When I asked for help, I was usually given bad help, met with silence, or told I needed to work it out on my own. So I could not fathom the world of a person who felt it was okay to ask for help, felt entitled to support, or could put off work they didn't understand or want to do. At times I would have judgmental thoughts about such people but secretly envied them for having a freedom I did not. Taking over and doing the work for others did not serve them or me—as I burnt out, I started to resent everyone else in my life who had time to relax, go on vacations, or hang out with friends. Meanwhile, my weekends were filled with community work. I truly believed that if I worked hard enough, I could create the community I wanted, but I had no space to savor the community being offered. I behaved as though I was sprinting through the work and would get to rest once everything was done. But there is no end to work.

What I needed was to rethink this sprint in terms of being a long hike, one that could be slow and deliberate with moments of rest and occasional moments when rushing was useful. Working together, these twins sustain aliveness and presence over time and through changing fortunes. Both teach us to how to embrace change, transformation, and presence. Being seems to be the obvious teacher of this, with its guidance to relax our grip on the world. Yet we can become too fixated on being, avoiding the risks and drama of taking necessary action. Doing pushes us into change and uncertainty. It wakes us up, invigorates us, compels us to look at what we've been avoiding. Together they become the paradox of manifestation magic: engaging in the work of our will while giving up control over how it comes to fruition.

EXERCISE
Getting to Know the Twins of Engagement

Set aside forty minutes to an hour to get to know your experience of doing and being. Have tasks you need or want to accomplish that are not urgent. I encourage you to set a timer to let that help you contain and focus on each of the twins.

Start with being. Set a timer for twenty to thirty minutes and breathe. You could engage in a meditative practice, either sitting still or walking in a slow circle. You could also rest. Either way, notice how it is to be with no particular agenda, to witness yourself without attempting to fix or manage what arises. If you notice a restlessness, worry, or any impulse to tend to a task, acknowledge it but maintain your ease. When the timer is finished, notice how you feel and what you recall about the quality of the experience.

Then set another timer, and now dedicate this time to working on your tasks. Let yourself get involved with them. If you find yourself wanting to get distracted or zone out, acknowledge it and see if you can return to the activity. Notice how it is to be fully immersed in doing things. Notice if you want to do multiple things at once, or how it feels when one task is interrupted by another. When the timer is finished, notice how you feel and what you recall about the quality of the experience. For the next day, try to pay attention to when you are doing and when you are being.

Empty Mouths

Cultivating being allows us to receive the merits and energies of life. We need to be there to receive our manifestations, the love of others, and the blessings of our gods and spirits.

For years I would do rituals and move quickly on because if I tried to "feel if anything happened," I would get caught up in anxious questioning and self-doubt. Stepping out of that and assuming good outcomes was useful, but now I am learning how to receive. Being present and taking in allows for a deeper reception of what is offered than when we dismiss it or move too quickly. Breathing energy up to god soul, we can pause and imagine receiving the gift back. When we pray to the gods, we can pause to feel what is returned. It's the difference between a friendly rub on the shoulder and an hour-long massage. If the idea of this makes you uncomfortable, you are in good company! Receiving is intimate and vulnerable, which does not always feel okay or safe. If you can let yourself practice to the edge of your tolerance, over time you may feel more softness and ease in receiving.

Doing without being is like cooking a delicious meal and eating most of it before realizing you've hardly tasted it. It's a great tragedy to miss out on life because we were so busy doing it. This relates to our compulsive hungers, those longings that always consume but never feel satiated. Approval may be such a hunger—no matter who says we did a good job, or how many compliments we get, we may feel fraudulent. Appreciation, admiration, love, sensual pleasure, or power each have the potential to be such hungers—no matter how much we get, it's never enough. These hungers are cavernous mouths with no tongue to taste or belly to digest. Nourishment passes through them into the abyss, leaving them starving and voracious. The exquisite pain of hunger is intolerable, so our attention turns toward lack. We're unable to see how much love, validation, approval are offered us on a regular basis. When we do notice, parts of us dismiss it. "Of course they're pretending to feel that way, they're my friend." "Oh wow, I've fooled everybody."

Our efforts to satiate these hungers may become extreme and destructive. At their worst, these efforts follow the path of addiction, constantly consuming and seeking the next dose, heedless of the cost to our health and loved ones. We may lie to ourselves and others to get what we want. We may push people away before they can see the awful emptiness. We may take up more and more space, overshadowing others and punishing them for not being exactly what we want in any given moment. We may make ourselves incredibly small, hoping to be seen with favor but terrified to ask for it. These insatiable hungers tend to travel with exquisite sensitivities—not only the longing for praise but also feeling crushed by disapproval. Not only the desperation for attention but also feeling annihilated by invisibility.

I call these empty mouths because I imagine these hungers as disembodied mouths floating in space that devour what they seek with no capacity to digest and absorb their experiences. The hunger is never satisfied. For example, an empty mouth might devour experiences of power over others through demanding attention, respect, or getting our way. At the same time, this mouth panics or rages over even small moments of disrespect, weakness, powerlessness, or lack of control. We may have many empty mouths—and yours may look nothing like mine—but I will offer some examples to give you a sense of what they can look like: An empty mouth might constantly crave the validation of social status through seeking more and more markers of success like money, awards, rankings, titles while worrying constantly about being insignificant or cast out. Another empty mouth seeks to devour attention through constant acts of exuberance or aggression that elicit praise and laughter—or sometimes annoyance and anger—to choke back the horrible feeling of being invisible. An empty mouth might have an insatiable appetite for constant approval and reassurance to stave off the terror, emptiness, or despair of not being liked by others. One more empty mouth might consume knowledge and understanding through constant books, training, and education to stifle the horror of feeling incompetent and unprepared.

Should we identify ourselves with our empty mouths, we will lack perspective as we consume. Each time we'll think *this* is what we need to finally feel better—this person's attention, this much money, this promotion, this expensive car. We may hate these hungers, but the empty mouths are compulsive in their efforts to stifle their painful underlying feelings. Importantly, none of these hungers are intrinsically wrong. Each of them arises from basic needs—to belong, to feel valuable, to feel loved, to be seen and understood, to feel competent, to be respected. Yet some pain has caused a distortion that interferes with these needs. These mouths cannot connect what they consume to what within us truly needs the nourishment.

Being provides the digestive capacity to receive, take in, and disseminate nourishment through our souls. Bringing a spacious, loving heart to our hungers and efforts to consume acquaints us with both the suffering and the fulfillment of those desires. Stay the hand that wants to swat away the compliment and instead be with the longing. Help that part of you take in the praise, the attention, the validation, the love. These mouths will learn to trust you and become less desperate and voracious. When they're hungry, you feed them. When they're satiated, they are calm. Instead of playing elaborate games or trying to obey obscure rules about when it's okay to want what you want, get to the point and ask, for example, "Could you tell me one thing you love about me?" And pause to receive their response, to feel how it is to hear the answer.

EXERCISE

Ask and Receive

One of the most potent forms of magic I've learned, particularly for learning how to feed the empty mouths, is that of asking and receiving. It is both simple and one of the hardest practices of all.

With Humans

Step One: Get a sense of what you want. Do you want to go out to dinner? Do you want to be told how cute you look today? Do you want a hug? Do you want a blessing?

Step Two: Go to the person who can give you what you want.

Step Three: Tell that person what you want and ask if they can give it to you.

Step Four: Accept the response that is offered.

Step Five: If you receive what you want, stay with it for a moment. Take a deep breath. Sense into your body how it feels to get what you want. Notice without judgment what happens. It may be incredibly uncomfortable; an urge to push it away or run away. Stay with that, if you can, while receiving what you want.

If you do not receive what you want or parts of you feel that what is offered is inauthentic or hurtful, stay with this experience for a moment. Still any urge, briefly, to blame or attack the person you've asked. See if you can observe how it feels in your body not to get what you want, or to get it and realize you do not like it. Without judgment, notice what happens. Ask these sensations what they need from you.

Step Six: Reflect on this process. What have you learned about asking and receiving? What would you do differently? Can you try it again?

With Spirits

Pour a cup of water and set it before an image connected to a god or spirit with whom you have relationship. Make offerings as appropriate—at minimum, offer a prayer celebrating the virtues and powers of this being. Ask it to help you receive one of its virtues or powers. Imagine the being filling this water with a quality of this virtue—as light, or as vibration, or as energy, or as a subtle fluid. Wait until you feel the cup is full of this virtue, and then drink the water slowly. Feel the water becoming your body, and stay with your imagining of how the spiritual quality suffuses and enters you.

Flowing

When these twins of doing and being reconnect in love, the peacock that emerges is like the soaring of the hawk who glides across the valley, alternately beating its wings and holding its glide to ride the winds. Active and engaged, yet not wasting energy with unnecessary effort—only what is needed to stay on course. Researcher Mihaly Csikszentmihalyi identified the conditions of peak life experiences in a state that he named "flow," characterized by joyful absorption and loss of self-consciousness while engaging in a challenging, skill-based task with clear goals and feedback in which action and awareness become one.[25] In this state of concentration and challenging ease, we are nourished and fed rather than drained by activity. The distinctions between being and doing dissolve and it feels as though we are riding the current in perfect alignment, fully ourselves and fully immersed in this world.

Flowing need not look the same for each of us, and we can have preferred tendencies for experiencing this state. As a point of inquiry, I'd like to look at energetic tendencies we fall into when the twins come together in integration and flow. Each flowing mode offers its own mysteries, its own virtues, and its own vulnerabilities. Each flowing mode suffers when the peacock disintegrates and being wars against doing. In understanding and accepting our tendencies, we can make them work for us while avoiding their pitfalls. Our work is to find and celebrate our core tendency and

---

25. Mihaly Csikszentmihalyi, *Flow: The Psychology of Optimal Experience* (HarperCollins, 2008), 43–70.

then learn what is useful from the others. When we stop fighting what we will do regardless, life tends to go better.

To identify these energetic tendencies, I looked at the modality of signs in Western astrology. In astrology, the twelve signs of the zodiac express both element and modality. Three signs share one element, but each sign expresses it through a distinct modality—cardinal, mutable, or fixed. Here I have named them wave, tree, and bee. Though I will list the astrological signs corresponding to the core tendencies, you may find that your instinctive tendency differs from the modality of the sign in which your sun, moon, or ascendant is housed. Follow your own knowing in this regard.

After each tendency, I offer a practice to get to know its energy better. I encourage all of us to spend time with each tendency, for integrating the strengths of other tendencies gives us greater versatility. If you readily identify your core energy, start by practicing with that one to help you anchor into its energy. For each practice, set aside an hour or so on three separate days. These days do not have to be in the same week or month, but it's worthwhile to dedicate time to inhabit these modes and see what they offer you. I encourage you to turn off or quiet any electrical devices that would grab your attention and distract you from being in these practices, but you know best what you need for focus and connection. After each practice, take time to reflect and process what it was like for you. I recommend considering the following questions: Did you have an interesting experience? Did you find the mode hard to engage? What did you expect, and what actually happened?

Wave

Waves flow as forceful expressions of will that break, dissolve, and withdraw to gather power. The folks experiencing this energetic tendency are forces of nature who push projects forward, breaking apart stagnation and drawing others into their vision and efforts to manifest. Waves build power as they propel forward with drive and ambition but inevitably break against the shore—in completion of a major accomplishment, getting through the crisis, or hitting their limit. When this happens, all that force dissolves. Waves appear adrift, withdrawn, or aimless until a new idea spurs them to gather force for another volley. In a flowing state, waves attune to where their energy wants to go and follow it, delighting in the purpose of work, and then resting deeply when they are between efforts.

When in a state of disintegration, waves feel like a ball being thwacked across the tennis court, with being and doing holding the rackets. Doing is in its full power here with the wave's excitement in bringing something new to fruition. Disintegrated waves may hate the intensity of doing and resist the call of a new idea. Or they might love doing too much, perpetuating it for too long until they crash and being takes hold. These being states might feel boring at best, depressive and anxious at worst, suffused with the wave's fear of being a loser who will never have another inspiration. This valley almost mirrors the peak of how they feel in doing when they're on top of the world, exhilarated by will and terrified they might not pull it off.

Waves correspond to the cardinal modality of astrology, that which catalyzes and initiates, relating to the signs of Aries, Cancer, Libra, and Capricorn.

EXERCISE
Riding the Wave

On this day, set three or four goals for yourself. They could involve running errands, seeing friends, or experiences you want to have, such as "Talk to a stranger in a coffee shop" or "Find a good pair of jeans." Begin when you are ready, and pursue your goals. If you want to set a clear map for your journey and follow it to completion, go for it. If you want to wander a bit while keeping your goals in mind, that is also good. But know that in this time you've set aside, you've set certain tasks to accomplish, so do your best to complete them. When you are done, take time to rest and notice how it feels after so much activity.

Tree

Trees express deep presence and enormous energy for the daily efforts of maintenance and protection. As trees are not using their energy seeking the next interesting thing, they have great reserves for rooting deeply into their territory. Getting a tree to move is a costly endeavor. Trees draw people to them with their stillness and profound reach—folks want to be near them and rest in their shade, even when they envy the tree's power. In a flowing state, trees rejoice in who and where they are and make profound discoveries in what would otherwise seem common. They stretch to their fullest depth and breadth, gloriously taking up space, sending energy and encouragement to their allies through the roots. They are able to sustain effort over time and not be shy about needing support, nourishment, and rest.

In a state of disintegration, being tends to have the advantage. The tree has a tendency to resist change and cling to its being even when transformation might be necessary, or it may react with untenable doing when its virtues are not immediately accepted and celebrated. A disintegrated tree may waste energy in doing to try to prove its value to those who would not recognize it. Disintegrated trees might also fail to cultivate their networks and instead focus on what they need, forgetting to share their abundance.

Trees correspond to the fixed modality of astrology, that which sustains and maintains, relating to the signs of Taurus, Leo, Scorpio, and Aquarius.

EXERCISE

Rooting the Tree

On this day, to the extent you are able, pick a place where you can stay for the time you've set aside without being harassed by unwelcome intrusions like nosy people or law enforcement. It could be a natural setting, an urban setting, or an indoor space. But it should be a place where you can stay for a long time without being bothered. Be a witness and see what comes to you as you watch and inhabit this place. Pay attention to your neighbors and whatever else shares this space with you. Talk to the human or other-than-human beings who come to you. Say hello to the spirit of this space. You do not have to be completely still—you might want to read, knit, stretch, sunbathe, or have a picnic depending on where and when you're rooting. The goal is to stay in this one place for a long while and see what it is like.

Bee

Bees move according to a mercurial map, drawn here and there, making startling and inspiring connections and opportunities for cross-fertilization. They may have a clear objective but their path toward it is in constant revision. Bees are genuinely curious about the world and happy to let it reveal new experiences and opportunities to learn. The bee seems most at home in the flowing state, where being and doing blur into one. What bees do for rest and rejuvenation may look identical to what they do for work or education—read a book, learn a new skill, research interesting topics, make art, or talk to people. Following their intuition yields a genius that could not be planned.

In a state of disintegration, however, that blurring of being and doing makes it difficult for bees to recognize their motivations and needs in the moment. In other words, they may not see the difference between pleasure and effort, between rest and work, or not making sure their activity is meeting their current needs. This can make unmet needs act out in unexpected and disruptive ways to which the bee might be unconscious—making bold promises and then disappearing, or being friendly and seductive and then suddenly turning vicious and biting.

Bees correspond to the mutable modality of astrology, that which dissolves and shifts, relating to the signs of Gemini, Virgo, Sagittarius, and Pisces.

EXERCISE
Following the Bee

On this day, we will draw inspiration from the practice of the dérive. Guy Debord characterized the dérive as when "one or more persons during a certain period drop their relations, their work and leisure activities, and all their other usual motives for movement and action, and let themselves be drawn by the attractions of the terrain and the encounters they find there."[26] This practice is truly about wandering, and could happen in an urban neighborhood, a forest, a field, or any large space. Begin wherever you like, and notice what calls to you. Walk in a direction that feels interesting. If you become curious

---

26. Guy Debord, "Theory of the Dérive," Situationalist International Online, accessed February 1, 2023, https://www.cddc.vt.edu/sionline/si/theory.html.

about something you see, go explore it. If you want to sit in an unusual place, go with it. Enter through the wrong door if you're curious what that would be like.

Slowing Down

Cultivating flowing could look like engaging a basic practice with slow but sustained energy and concentration. The basics are the foundation upon which we grow and to which we continually return to grow in power. Without a strong base, growth is riskier and more prone to injury and accident. Moving slowly, with as much power as we can summon, helps us focus on technique and form, which is vital to an enduring practice. As beginners, we may resent the basics and moving slowly because we are eager to get to the power and the cool magic. We get frustrated with sitting and breathing for ten minutes, or visualizing a spinning cube, or saying the same prayers every single day. Yet as magic gets more complex and advanced, we get lost without those basics. We start fighting astral demons and posting vague, threatening social media messages about the people we imagine to be cursing us instead of doing a cleansing of the house and resetting the wards. We get lost in our fantasies and fears instead of being able to remember that state of presence that comes from slow, deliberate breathing. We imagine our problems to be insurmountably complex instead of using our tools to break them down into their simplest forms.

If you work out with weights, for example, it's important to learn proper form and lift enough weight to be challenged but not compromise form. Going too heavy too quickly and compromising posture is a great way to injure yourself. Even if you don't pull a muscle, other subtle injuries form over time from bad form. Then we must add rest and recovery time and humble ourselves to go down several weights back to our level of basic competence.

Finding the edge of competence, or slightly past it, lets us push to exhaustion within our tolerance. Then we rest, recover, and do it again—and if the edge of competence is further out, we work there.

It is so tempting to get ensnared by impatience, to want to rush over the problem rather than slow down and inhabit it. From that tense, impatient place, bad magic tends to come. I'll turn to my pendulum and ask it for clarity only to find its answers conflicting and confounding. Mostly because my questions are not clear, and my energy too unfocused. When I get the most lost in my magical practice, or caught up in my anxieties and worries, nothing helps more than slowing down my breathing and expanding my belly as I inhale and exhale.

EXERCISE
Back to Basics

Think of a magical practice that you consider foundational, one that you've done dozens if not hundreds of times, and dedicate a week to doing it daily, but taking it much slower than you would normally. You might do this with banishing, circle casting, divination, meditation, or breathing exercises. If you say a daily prayer, for example, try slowly intoning the words and pausing between each statement for a full and complete inhalation and exhalation. Notice how the prayer resonates in your body and what comes up in your soul. When you practice slowly, try to bring as much presence and vigor as you would to a normal practice, but lengthen and extend your time engaged with it, like you're doing it in half-time slow motion. Journal about how it goes. What feels challenging about being slow and powerful? Does it illuminate anything useful that could enhance your work? How is it to try to stay present when moving slowly?

Chapter 8

TRAPS AND FEAR

To stay on this path, we need enough confidence in ourselves to keep moving forward with a willingness to let all we believe be tested and refined. Though there is continuity of awareness, the you who casts the spell is not the you who will receive its fruits. What feels urgent and precious in the moment later becomes unimportant or even a hindrance to further development as a magic worker. So it is that the manifestation of our dreams could become a pair of steel jaws clamped around our leg that needs to be pried apart and discarded if we're to continue. I've seen people run into situations that look ideal only to find themselves ensnared. Once, I had a friend whose dream it was to relocate to a different country. They took the risk to move and asked for my magical aid. I sensed they would need a strong community, connection to family, and legal and financial support to succeed, so I did a working to this end. What followed seemed like a dream, including a handsome lover willing to help my friend marry into citizenship. Over time, however, troubling details emerged: texts about bad fights between them, the lover's increasingly con-trolling demands on my friend's time and emotions, his jealousy if my friend spent time with anyone else, offhand comments about my friend being hit when their lover was too anxious and upset. My friend showed a number of signs of a victim of domestic violence—

blaming themself for the controlling behavior and abuse, distressed when I introduced the word "abuse" into the conversation.

A trap is only a trap when you want to leave. Before that, a trap may be a home, a paradise, a job, or a meaningful relationship. Only when we realize things are untenable and we want out do we discover how stuck we are. Desire lures us in, and fear holds us. Struggling against the snares makes them grow tighter, but collapsing in horror and despair doesn't serve our escape. Neither does resignation turn that trap back into a home. We may find ourselves trapped in abusive or empty relationships; in loneliness; in untenable workplace conditions; in financial debt; in communities that were once wonderful and now feel toxic; and within our own intractable patterns. In my friend's case, they were caught in physical and emotional patterns of control of which I likely only knew surface details, but the sharper teeth of their abuser's grip controlled my friend's citizenship and access to healthcare, aid, and support. I know them to be an incredibly resilient person, but they were isolated and vulnerable.

The inability to imagine a clear path of escape is a major sign of being trapped. You can sit with a person who's stuck and go through every possible scenario of change. No matter how promising it seems, they'll sigh and explain why it couldn't work. Invisible ropes bind them in every direction—if they pull left, the right grows tighter. It's frustrating to sit with—it's frustrating for the stuck person, too. It's not a failing of will but a common emotional response to living with a situation for too long from which escape will be costly. We fear a future that's worse than the present. These conditions bind our capacity to imagine what is possible and limit the potency of magic. When it's time to dare, we flinch before the casting and thus send out a weaker spell. Our parts fight each other instead of aligning in shared purpose, entangled by confusion, doubt, and discord. The hope for better feels too distant. Usually the trapped person's fears of the future are projections of their present life—getting more stuck financially or emotionally, or feeling alone. If you're trying to help, it doesn't work to tell them these fears are silly or unfounded. What proof do you have that is more compelling than the evidence they're living? We cannot promise a better future, and vague hopes look unconvincing next to the evidence of life as it is. If you want to empower a trapped person to take the risk, start by appreciating their fears and telling them what support you can offer.

One snare that keeps us trapped is trying to hold on to too much. Our true desire hangs slightly out of reach, and we keep thinking one day we'll have it and be free of the harm. This is one way of understanding the earnest efforts someone being abused may take to placate their abuser—often abusers are capable of extraordinary sweetness and love, and their victims become convinced they could turn the relationship back to that bliss. If they clutch the love and sweetness of a partner, the hope is that the horrible behavior goes away. If we grasp the money and social status afforded by a job, the hope is that its demands will relinquish enough to let us enjoy these things, one day. We're attached to an image of ourselves as a person who is good, or never gets angry, or is too smart to be in this position, and our unwillingness to let go of that keeps us playing another person's game. For some traps, leaving means putting our actual lives in danger.

Two moves are important for escaping the trap. The first is to recognize the situation for what it is, and take a moment to stop fighting. This is not resignation—it is getting a calm and sober assessment of reality. The next move is to assess what we are willing to sacrifice for freedom. This is a harsh thought. We need to measure the cost of sacrifice against the total daily misery of living in this trap. What is your freedom worth? If the sacrifice is too costly, then what could be possible to bring you back into power in this situation? My friend eventually escaped, aided by the fortuitous relocation of close family nearby. They risked their citizenship and safety to get away and eventually landed in exactly the conditions for which I'd worked in my magical support—good work, stable citizenship, family and friends nearby, and mutual love. This magic was much slower and more fraught than I would have liked.

By telling this story, it's not my intent to take credit for my friend's courage in escaping a horrible situation nor blame for their falling into it. It's to remind us that though escape may seem impossible and hope a fool's snare, you have access to magic, no matter your circumstances. Magic has existed in myriad forms in nearly all cultures, classes, and caste positions. Poor, immigrant, and enslaved people have always had magic for protection against physical and legal violence, for birth control, treating illness, and holding their families together. Wealthy, powerful people have always had magic for advancing their political interests, building and breaking alliances, and discerning times for war. Political and economic favor aids magic, but magic has always been available to the dispossessed and those without privilege and influence. Power arises from inner spiritual strength, a robust network of spirit supports, and the recognition of community. Whether you work with tools you've bought at great price, forged by hand, or drawn on pieces of paper—you have all you need. When we cannot see a way out, that is a perfect moment for magic. In this chapter, we will look at some common beliefs that lead us into traps. Attend to any that you recognize in your life, and remember your power.

The Trap of Too Much Control

When I started practicing martial arts late in life, I had a lot of fear of getting hurt and even more of hurting others. I tried to learn the moves with weaker force, thinking that once my body knew what to do, I could try being more forceful. My practice was rigid and tentative. My sensei started calling me out on it. Though I performed the actions, I was not bringing the force and commitment to truly practice aikido. There was no aliveness in my movements, only control. To make progress, I needed softness and vigor. One day, as Sensei observed my weapons work, he challenged me to give up control and strike with greater power. It would feel wild and scary at first, he noted, but it would help me grow in both power and control. This was a revelation. For so long, control arrested power within me to prevent it from exploding and causing harm. I'd never considered that power and control could support each other. To my surprise, bringing more intensity into my attacks created more safety for myself and others. An instinct and bodily intelligence emerged that I had never experienced before; I was able to respond to peril without being slowed by my anxious, overthinking brain.

Bringing that insight into my magical practice, I see how those same fears of power and hurting self or others impeded my spellwork. Whenever I had a bold desire, I would mitigate it with a prayer of doing no harm or making sure the results would be to the benefit of all beings. Ethically, this is a sound aspiration—a wish that both causes harm and benefits few seems like a terrible idea. Yet I wonder to what extent this is the magical expression of people-pleasing behaviors, making the self small to avoid feeling guilty and provoking the anger of others. "I call upon the great and powerful spirits to come to my aid and bring me my heart's desire…if that's okay. No worries if not."

The material of this trap is the fantasy of how much control we have over life, baited with the hope that vigilant attention will prevent harm befalling ourselves or others. This has the psychological flavor of what in developmental psychology is called "magical thinking." Kids around the age of toddlerhood tend to go through a period of believing that their thoughts and actions have power over the world in ways that adults would find misguided. When I was a kid, I would see a plane flying through the air and have the sudden and terrifying fear that it would explode if I imagined it to happen, which of course meant that I imagined it exploding while fearing I would cause an explosion. Wielding that kind of power would be terrifying, given how little control we have over our thoughts.

When we turn toward a magical practice in adulthood, we must in part take what is necessary from that cognitive stage and leave behind what is problematic. We must believe that we can cause change through our will and imagination while recognizing the limits of our power. I've known people who feared they got entire flights canceled because they upset a god, or were terrified of doing magic for what they wanted for fear of achieving their desires through the harm of others. It is not for me to say whether these stories are valid. I do think believing such stories implicitly positions one as the main character of the world, in which everything that occurs is about you. This renders the billions of other humans and lifeforms and spirits sharing this existence with you as will-less side characters with no power of their own, no gods looking after their interests. Yet we are all of God Herself.

Doing magic adds a dash of generative chaos into our lives, making it possible for manifestations to come in unexpected ways that make complete sense in retrospect. Hence, we share common wisdom to craft an intention so that you are clear about what you want but vague about how you get it. Instead of casting to get *this* specific job opportunity from *this* company, you craft an intention for a job that meets your needs and requirements and then stay open to what comes your way. This practice alone creates safety in manifesting desires without causing harm to people. Magic tends to follow paths of least resistance, and it's much more energy and effort to cause harm than to bring together unexpected harmonies. Another good practice is regular prayer and offerings to our gods, ancestors, or other spirit allies, asking them to look after us and keep us from turning evil. And it is also good practice to learn to apologize, make amends, and repair harm when it's caused. Instead of seeing harm as this horrible damning thing, we need to accept it as the risk of coming into power. Our power is better served in making things right when they go wrong rather than tying ourselves in knots with the fear of unintended consequences.

Spending too much effort to control whether, when, and how our manifestation occurs is like keeping our hands gripped tightly to everything we're trying to fix in place. There's no room for desire. Our hands need to be open and empty, ready to receive what God Herself offers. Magic pries things from our grip that no longer serve. There is little in life that we control, even those of us with great power. These days, when I have a problem with no obvious solution that is taking up too much mental space, I see an opportunity to do magic and see what happens. It keeps things interesting!

The Trap of Being the Chosen One

When I was in high school, I was a fan of the television show *Buffy the Vampire Slayer*. If you are unfamiliar with the concept, the main character Buffy is a high school aged young woman who inherits a lineage of great strength and power along with the mandate to protect the living against the forces of evil, primarily vampires. *Buffy* is one example of a common fantasy trope, the "chosen one." One might see this as an example of the archetypal story that Joseph Campbell called "the hero's journey," in which a person is called to go on an adventure, experience transformation, and then bring that power back home. Where the "chosen one" mythology differs is that it's not about an average person pulled into events larger than life. Chosen ones are set apart as special and with unique gifts, prophecies, or supernatural blessings that separate them permanently and inescapably from all others. Though all Buffy wanted was to have a regular high school life, as she often protested, danger would be drawn to her. Though she hated the crushing burden of responsibility for having the powers she had, she was frequently told and came to believe that no one else was strong enough to do what needed to be done. In the hero's journey, one could refuse the call of adventure, but the chosen one cannot do so without bearing responsibility for the victory of evil. The special powers and undeniable sense of important purpose is the bait of this trap, while its harm is the accompanying life of isolation, misunderstanding, vilification, and compulsion to make horrible choices. The chosen one is inflated in a cosmic sense of importance while simultaneously being made disposable, a sacrifice in the war against evil with no recourse to retire except for death.

In our spiritual lives, many of us long to be a chosen one. We may be craving the important message, ready to seize on any deep purpose that becomes apparent. Even if it makes no sense. Even if it hurts us. My own magical journey has been gradual and slow, beset by doubts and confusion. Meanwhile I saw colleagues having sudden and undeniable spiritual experiences that disrupted their lives. A part of me envied what looked like spiritual certainty and specialness. But the consequences of these experiences were unsettling and needing of care—exacerbation of mental illnesses, eruption of physical problems, and ruptures in community and relationship that came as they integrated this new piece of spiritual reality into their lives.

Through a psychological lens, those of us who instinctively relate to the chosen one story may have been forced into adult roles at a young age. Maybe we had to emotionally, physically, or financially care for our parents and siblings. Maybe we had to protect ourselves when no one else would. These experiences instilled in us the sense of having an enormous responsibility bigger than our capacity to handle yet impossible to refuse for fear of horrible things occurring. The chosen one mythology also emerges from alienation. When we are in a community where we know our place and value, we don't need to feel set apart and exalted. We don't have to live in a world where we carry everything alone. But when we do live in isolation and not-belonging, the idea of being special, powerful, and indispensable is appealing. Who could reject us when they depend upon us? Inhabiting that role perpetuates loneliness. Others do not relate to us as friends and equals. Sharing our burdens would suddenly erase our whole story of worth. So we are both inflated and deflated.

Through a political lens, the chosen one reflects ambivalence about empire. To become an empire requires devotion to the importance of one's own culture and government, requiring submission and absorption from the cultures we dominate. How can we justify ourselves as moral and worthy while subjugating others? Tell a story about being specially chosen to rule and protect the weak. Add that we are divinely favored to protect the world from a horrible ill, and to be the bringer of what we call virtues, like civilization, or a particular religion, or a form of government. Through a spiritual lens, the chosen one mythology expresses our longing to know our purpose in life, what we uniquely offer to the world.

Without grounding in familial or cultural traditions, a community of belonging, or a deep relationship to land, this longing is vulnerable to exploitation by charismatic beings with a story of our specialness. It feels so good to be seen and valued, to be inflated by our specialness. It becomes a drug. We do anything to hold onto that. This is the bait of the trap that locks us in painful, abusive relationships; cult dynamics; and abusive experiences with spirit.

At its most benign, being the chosen one impedes our development and the work of slow magic. When we come to believe we are the only ones who do it, that everything would fall apart without us, we are no longer free to align our wills and follow desires that would take us away from this burden. Feelings of obligation and duty calcify and become the ruling principle of life. We cannot grow, move on, or allow others the space to grow into these responsibilities thrust upon us. What once was passion becomes resentment; what once was earnest service becomes self-sacrificing martyrdom. Yet it is all grounded in a falsehood. There is no one person so special that they alone must bear all responsibilities. People have a genius for caring for themselves in ways we cannot predict or expect. Visions and great ideas exist in the world beyond us, seeking those ready and able to bring them into being. If you decide you cannot do a great vision justice and let it pass, it will move on to another, and they can decide if it is their task. The world will not lose those visions, so you are free to follow your path.

The Trap of Too Much Credulity

The world of spirits is as varied and full of agendas as the human world. There is no unambiguously benevolent god or spirit whose messages are beyond dispute. Beings come in glory promising great things, but they may be feeding off our suffering and stress. Even the gods who love us may be met with discernment.[27] While their perspectives are more vast, seeing what we cannot, there are things we may see that they do not. Gods may not appreciate our human needs, limits, and conflicts. We may need to remind our gods that we need to sleep at night or make money to survive and cannot dedicate all our time and energy to their tasks. In our deepening relationships, we may experience personal gnosis of the gods that is useful for our practice but not widely accepted. If working with that gnosis brings us health, vitality, and integrity, it is not necessary for others to know or accept our beliefs. There are times, however, when our gnosis brings harm and disintegration.

What we experience with a spirit may say more about the part of us we are seeing through than the nature of the spirit. Occasionally I encounter spirits or gods who seem to confirm hurtful and disempowering stories about me. Or they may offer inflating, wish-fulfilling stories that I want to believe. When I check and set aside the hopes and fears I'm bringing to the moment, the spirit's message changes. They may reveal themselves as tricksters or frauds. They may have a wholly different message distorted by my biases. Martial gods in particular seem to enjoy goading until told to back off, because they want us strong. What matters is practicing discernment and grounding yourself in a basic sense of humanity and goodness. We all have struggles, and strengths and weaknesses, and we can all cause hurt to each other and need to make amends. But if what your spirits say to you seems to be too good (or too awful) to be true, be wary. Check in with yourself. Call upon your guides and higher self or take the tools of your power and ask the

---

27. I write in more depth about discernment practice in Pagan and Polytheist contexts in the "Passion Exalted in Wisdom" chapter of my book *Circling the Star* (Gods & Radicals, 2018), 99–112.

spirit to reveal what it truly is. We will explore practices for this later in the book.

The Trap of Pretending Reality is Not Real

Abraham-Hicks, a proponent of the "Law of Attraction," is Esther Hicks channeling an extra-dimensional consciousness known as Abraham. In a 2008 clip, a Black woman asks for advice on explaining to her young son the legacy of racism and white supremacy in the United States, specifically in view of his school's upcoming lesson about Martin Luther King, Jr.[28] Abraham-Hicks chides this woman about her son "feeling bad" about the things the woman and her mother and grandmother "felt bad about." The questioner, clearly valuing Abraham-Hicks's work and teachings, politely points out that her son will encounter racism regardless of what she says or does not say.

Abraham-Hicks's response takes Dr. King's legacy of strident nonviolent activism against segregation and poverty and turns it into what she calls the "empowered version." In this telling, Dr. King's dream captivated and inspired those who listened so long as he remained in alignment. When he tried to "push against the stream" to make his dream reality, however, it caused "abrupt things to happen." The phrasing is roomy enough to include, without naming, Dr. King's assassination and the violence perpetrated upon civil rights activists from police batons, incarceration, firehoses, and civilian assaults. All abrupt things! With this "empowered version," Abraham-Hicks suggests the Black mother summarize the activist's work by saying Dr. King "saw injustice that I don't want to talk about," to avoid making her son "feel bad."

---

28. Abraham-Hicks, "Abraham on Martin Luther King," March 6, 2008, https://www .youtube.com/watch?v=kBB5UzdO5es.

According to the Law of Attraction in its popular form, talking about injustice and violence pollutes one's consciousness and draws the experience toward any who do. The idea is that to manifest what you truly desire, you need to purify your consciousness so your thoughts are only toward and within the reality you wish to inhabit. If you don't want injustice and violence, you don't talk about it, don't think about it, don't feel bad about it. This version is palatable and soothing to those of us who are not targets of the injustice and violence in question. It lets us avoid the discomfort of challenging and rectifying those conditions. King himself contended with an early version of this perspective in his day, with white moderates worried he was moving too quickly and pushing too hard for change. He bemoaned this as a great "stumbling-block" to racial justice coming from the white moderate "who prefers a negative peace which is the absence of tension to a positive peace which is the presence of justice."[29]

On the path of slow magic, we might similarly want to close our eyes to unpleasant truths in favor of focusing on the reality we desire. Successes in life might entice us to close our hearts to those suffering around us, instead admonishing them to do their own work without support. The growth of power within, unbalanced by cultivating right-sized pride and compassion, makes it hard to see validity in vulnerability and victimhood. We may think that others' focus on their own suffering seems to magnify it, and so we decide to ignore suffering altogether. Many a magical practitioner has argued that oppressed peoples manifest their own suffering through the Law of Attraction, drawing discrimination toward them through their belief in it. It's worth considering that the civil

---

29. Martin Luther King, Jr, "The Negro Is Your Brother," *The Atlantic Monthly* 212, no. 2 (August 1963): 78–88. Accessed November 27, 2023, https://www.theatlantic.com /magazine/archive/1963/08/the-negro-is-your-brother/658583/.

rights movement was an exemplary magical working. Those nonviolent activists with whom Dr. King was aligned spent hours practicing with each other the skills of reacting calmly and nonviolently to intense and violent provocation. It was a discipline they cultivated so that when it came time for direct action, they were ready. Their behavior was the Law of Attraction *par excellence*—instead of believing in a world of segregation and violence, they acted as if living in the world they desired. They sat calmly in sections designated for white people only. Decades later, Black people rallied under the powerful, clear intention that "Black lives matter." And yet both generations experienced violent resistance. How could bigotry and violence find them when living in such alignment?

The individual will is not the prime mover of reality, and the singular conscious is not the architect of the world. We live in a world of a multiplicity of wills interacting in a vast ecosystem. Racial bias lives within the mind of the oppressor as much as, if not more than, the mind of the oppressed. Should the oppressed challenge the comfort of dominance, it is the oppressor's unchecked anger and frailty that brings forth violence. The oppressor enacts violent laws. The oppressor sends police and military to do violence on their behalf. Sometimes the oppressor does violence with their own hands. Consider that no one goes to the police and military to preach about the Law of Attraction, exhorting them to suppress all thoughts of danger and violence and focus instead on love, light, and harmony while engaging with adversaries.

Each of us inhabits two worlds. One world is wholly yours: your thoughts, your feelings, your story, and your perceptions. That world is yours to tend. The other world we share with each other and with multitudinous life forms and beings. Our presence influences this world, but it existed before us and will persist beyond us. Our ancestors did not survive in the outer world by ignoring predators in the shadows and focusing their inner worlds on the manifestation of food. We need full, soft awareness to inhabit both worlds at once. We can center desire in our focus, but our physical senses need to be receptive to what's happening around us. To do the great working of changing a society—the slowest and most profound magic of all—we must be able to name the violent and oppressive conditions we face, and recognize the threat of retaliation when those conditions are challenged.

Fear

Fear is normal when undertaking a major work. Yet you may not think of yourself as being fearful. Do you ever worry? Do you ever feel concerned? Do you ever anticipate what has, could, or will go wrong? For the purposes of this section, consider all of those experiences to be included in the category of "fear." Some try to bolster us against fear by saying it is irrational and best ignored, ridiculed, or dismissed, but I find this unhelpful. Should we allow ourselves to name our fears, they make complete sense. They may be grounded in things we've experienced in our lives, so it's unconvincing to tell yourself it could never happen. It has! We may fear getting horribly sick, bullied, losing our income, losing important friendships and relationships, or being attacked. Those fears are rational!

Fear is powerful. When it's not our ally, it throws off our aim or blocks us from acting. When we don't take the concerns of our scared parts seriously, they won't trust us. Without trust, they will thwart our actions. Once again, the people and parts who "sabotage" us lack agency. When given a voice and a vote, they're invested. So I advocate listening to our fear. Lifting it from the burial ground of the unconscious and giving it language, speaking it into the air, or writing it on a sheet. You might worry this naming will invite what you fear. I find naming to be a dispelling. Naming the scary thing allows the fear to step outside of me. When fear is inside, it sounds horrifyingly convincing. On the outside, we can see with perspective and clarity. We can assess the likelihood of threat alongside the potential severity of consequences. It might be that we decide the opportunity is worth the risk. Or we might, calmly and deliberately, decide it is not, and explore how else to pursue desire. It's useful to ground and center yourself before naming your fears with as much compassion and generosity as you can, not to belittle or apologize for them, but to risk complete honesty with yourself. Once our fears are named, we have more clarity about how to leave the trap.

EXERCISE
Plotting Your Escape from a Trap

These instructions are for a divinatory or reflective journaling practice, but if you have a trusted person you can partner with, it's particularly powerful to let them ask you the questions and witness your responses. I'd encourage the witness not to add any commentary, criticism, or encouragement—listen to what is being said and repeat back what is heard until the speaker feels understood.

Spend a few minutes focusing on your breathing and your state of being. Notice the stability of the ground and breathe that stability into your body. As you exhale, let all of yourself relax and let the ground take more of your weight. Let any part of you that needs stability or ease take in the sensation of being completely supported by the ground. Think of a situation in life in which you feel trapped or a time when you've felt trapped. If it's the latter, do this exercise as a past tense reflection on that experience.

Do divination or reflective journaling with these questions: What desire keeps me in this trap? What paths are available for me to escape this trap? What do I fear could happen if I followed the path out? (If you have identified multiple paths, answer for each.) What do these fears need to become my allies?

Once complete, contemplate a piece of magic you can do to honor your answer to the last question. If you drew a card or rune, you could take a photo of it and keep it on your home screen. You could create a sigil or a charm bag signifying the work to make fear into your ally. You could cast a circle and call upon the spirit of your fear to talk with it. You could burn a candle infused with the energy of this transformation. Then see what happens.

Chapter 9

Working with Spirit

We do not make magic in controlled circumstances. Our efforts contend with the weather. Currents of wind and water help and hinder the ship sailing across the water. So too do subtle spiritual currents affect our magic. From the small fae who spoils the milk out of spite to the vast elemental guardian offering skill and gnosis, spirits may aid or hinder our workings. While some of these spirits embody the primal forces of the currents themselves, others teach us to read and divine the weather in which we work our magic. With practice, we may learn to master these currents, but adapting skillfully is more than enough for a life's work.

Spirit work confronts us with our tendencies about connection and dependence upon others. Even if you grew up sensing the presence of other beings in the world, you may share the story that we're on our own in this world. That aloneness births joy and horror—the joy of feeling strong and independent mastery of the world; the horror of living in an overwhelming world with no one looking out for us. Even if we hate that aloneness, we may feel averse to giving up independence. We may fear disappointment, abandonment, or rejection in our time of greatest need and so avoid any dependence at all. Rejecting the community of spirits, we might cling to self-work as a strategy of control to stave off the terrors of inferiority and shore up this idea that we are one lone, bounded, solitary being. Should we be willing to face and walk through these fears, true belonging lies on the other side.

Authenticity is not a vial of precious chemicals that must be sealed off to remain pure. It is a flower in an enormous meadow, open to pollination from unexpected allies. It is fed by those we admire and despise, those who teach us and guide us, and those who warn us. Where our powers reach their limits, others can support us with their skills and perspectives. Our community of people, spirits, and other lifeforms can lend us aid to correct our missteps, watch our backs, and tend what we cannot manage, all of which are invaluable on a slow magic path. In the moments when we feel exhausted of strength and despairing of will, allies carry us through the door of change into a deeper level of power and understanding. Spirits see what we're unable to recognize and bring our attention to what we'd otherwise miss. Allies keep us safe from the dangers we don't always sense, especially from other spirits whose energy and intentions are not healthy for us.

An alliance is a mutual relationship of shared goals and interests. So much of magic is about being in good relationships with other beings. No matter how tough and powerful you are, it helps to be on good terms with your neighbors and have friends who care about your well-being. Even casual, transactional relationships are of use from time to time. Spirits enable power we could not harness on our own. They illuminate patterns that we are too close to recognize. A large community increases our access to a diversity of protection, resources, and support. When we only work with spirits of compassion and love, we may struggle in situations that demand vigor and assertiveness. It is useful to have friends and allies who are strong where we feel weak.

Spirit Etiquette

When clients take me on as their therapist we have an explicit contract: I provide witnessing, attention, and support, but in return I must be paid. Within this relationship there is deep caring and connection, but it does not work without transparency and clear expectations on the transactional agreements that contain our work. Once upon a time, I offered this depth of listening and care to almost anyone, burning with idealistic fervor that the world would be so much better if everyone was this way all the time. But in the world as it is, I gave out far more than I received. Once the work became my primary source of income, I needed to become colder. I couldn't generously give this level of attention to everyone while stressing over how to pay for my housing, utilities, food, medical care—all the normal costs of life. Now I am clearer about the relationships I'm willing to offer this care to, and under what conditions. For those I love, who offer that level of care and attention without demand, I am more than happy to give in turn. Mutuality is a necessity for any healthy relationship. With strangers, we can be transactional. For those we love and cherish, it's not so much about keeping score as feeling that we're both getting from the relationship as much as we're giving to it without it being a constant fight to be valued. Giving and receiving keeps relationships vibrant. Relationships with spirits are not much different.

Spirits can and do engage in transactional work and may be inclined to help a beginner on the path, but long-term relationships require tending. When we honor the spirits regularly, check in on them, and do things for them without always demanding their aid, we may receive great blessing and care without a steep cost. When we fail to approach the spirits except with a demand or another crisis and invest little into the relationship, their interest and trust erodes. If you know the rules, manners, and expectations of human relationships, you can usually apply those to your spirit relationships to good effect. The behavior of a good houseguest is good to follow in spirit relationships—including making the effort to ask when you do not know what is wanted. Certain realms have particular etiquette (one notorious example is the fae) but it is true of all cultures. In some households, failing to remove your shoes upon entering is rude, whereas in other households it would be strange if you walked around barefooted. The larger lesson is to learn the customs and etiquette of the home you are visiting and abide by their ways when entering their territory.

Sensing Spirits

For years, my expectations of spirit communication were misguided. When folks talked about hearing or seeing, I thought that meant all the "real" psychics perceived with their physical eyes and ears. Elders of mine would become distracted mid-conversation by spirit messages, as if the gods always stood at their shoulder, whispering in their ears. Nothing like that happened for me. All I thought I "heard" was silence. The vivid experiences I had in my imagination I assumed were mere projections of expectations and hopes. Pushing them away, I waited for the true message. After several years it occurred to me that I might be ignoring the true messages. Once I became curious about these seemingly irrelevant fantasies, my spiritual life began to open up with more potency and nuance.

The imagination is a faculty of soul akin to the wireless network connecting our personal "devices" to a much larger field of intelligence. Experiences of trance and dream show how the imagination is a realm where the unexpected occurs beyond the expectations of our day-to-day ego. There is occasional debate in magical communities as to whether these practices are contacting "real" spirits or if it's "just" your own personal psychology. Working with parts of self has settled me into a certainty of there being a spiritual world beyond my personal psychology. Yet seeking to define a precise distinction between the two is like trying to mark where the beach ends and the ocean begins. When imagined experience is shallow, effortful, and anxious, we are likely still on the beach, where various parts are usually mediating the spirit contact through their anxieties, fears, and fantasies. The more we come into a state of calm relaxation, soothing our distressed parts and letting them settle, the more we deepen into the ocean, making contact with what is beyond the self. After several minutes, if we are able to stay focused and keep relaxing, unexpected things begin to happen in the imagination. Figures begin speaking on their own, offering new thoughts and images that surprise and move us.

The ritual protocols of magic facilitate getting into this state of relaxation. Deep breathing, sending roots into the ground, purifying the space with incense or salt water, and creating sacred space all help us to slow down and deepen from a superficial and stressed state of consciousness into a state closer to our expansive dreaming soul that's able to hold vast complex experiences without becoming tense or brittle. Practicing the longer, structured ceremonies trains us so that we may drop into those states more quickly as needed. Not all of us imagine the same way. We may not have inner monologues, or cannot imagine visually. There is usually a quality of sensing available to us, if only sudden and unexpected knowledge. To an extent, we cultivate these faculties through visualization practices—trying to imagine what it's like to see, smell, feel, taste, or hear an experience we've known through our physical senses.

Awakening psychic awareness and spirit contact thrives with listening to and following the guidance of these experiences as they come through. Being cautious, however, is wise—the sharpest psychic senses may be misled or receive a fraction of what we need to know. It is worthwhile to explore, experiment, and test out what comes through. I was once given homework to connect with an herbal ally, and I befriended rosemary. As I listened, the spirit of rosemary suggested it would be good as a tea for countering inflammation. When I shared this with my more herbally informed community, they added the caution to drink such a tea in moderation because it also induces vomiting and may harm those with liver disease. Similarly, it's good to check that the rosemary you're using is in good condition and not harboring any unwanted pests or chemicals that would cause other health risks. Embracing magic and nature does not require throwing out all critical thought.

EXERCISE

Listening to a Spirit

The following exercise is written with the intent of building relationship with a benign spirit. Should you wish to work with notoriously dangerous or chaotic spirits (like demons), you will want more complex layers of protection, such as putting the representative sigil or object in a separate protective circle. For any spirit, I'd recommend keeping a tool at hand such as a wand or blade that bears your power and ability to protect yourself.

Here is a simple practice: Sit or stand near a place, object, or representation of the spirit. If you create sacred space through casting a circle or clearing the energies of your space, it's worthwhile to do so. Then call in the spirit you wish to engage with through extemporaneous speech, visualization, or breathing out an invitation through your heart. Wait, breathe, and notice what happens. Attend to any shifts in your body, your thoughts, your mood, the environment. Observe any visuals or words that come through. Ask questions to understand the spirit better and wait for an answer. That is, don't try to figure out the answers; instead, make an effort to ask and wait for an answer to come. Hold whatever comes up in your experience as connected to that answer.

If the spirit overwhelms or distresses you, check in with yourself and ask if this is coming from the spirit or a part of you experiencing the distress. If you sense it's a part, ask what the part needs, and see if you can support it in coming to a calm, relaxed place. If it needs to stop for today, honor that and stop. Ask the part what would help it feel ready to try again later. If the part is able to calm and give you space, turn back and see if your experience of the spirit changes. Finally, ask the spirit for a practice to continue getting to know it and see what comes. Then thank the spirit and send it away, asking it to give you space and go to where it wants to be. Cleanse your space again or close your circle.

Building Trust

Even when I felt I was able to contact a spirit, at times I felt blocked in "hearing" what was being said to me. A god would open her mouth and noise obscured her words. Something in me inhibited the message, fearing it would cause suffering—the god would demand too much of me, be cruel or critical, compel me to change everything. The inhibiting part might point out, rightly, that I was at my limit in life and did not have room for another revolution, another upheaval. My greatest fear in listening to spirits was losing control and autonomy, a fear rooted in the messages I internalized from Catholicism, which considered its god and angels infallible, their edicts to be followed without question. Other spirits were suspect, potential demons who would jeopardize my soul with eternal damnation. What's more, those who claimed to speak for the infallible divine told me my nature was objectively disordered; my truth was marked with sin, threatening eternal consequences. Yet as sincerely as I tried to practice their way, the mental and emotional consequences were enormous. Denying my truth to live theirs would have led me to self-destruction. The stakes of spirit contact were high!

Anchoring to a more affirming religion, I still craved connection to a beneficent god who would accept and guide me to who I was supposed to be in the world. Within me was a set of devotional divine twins: one resisting the loss of autonomy, the other yearning to surrender in total devotion. The surrendering twin within me imagined the right god or spirit would finally give me the purpose and certainty I craved while removing doubt. The gods have always refused this twin's entreaties. The autonomous twin within me mistrusts the agendas of any other being, spirit or human. No wonder there was resistance. With practice, those twins have softened in their war against each other to open the way for the path between. Like people, spirits have their own agendas, perspectives, strengths, and limits. While some are antagonistic toward humans, a spirit does not need to feel malice to cause you harm. Harm may befall us from a spirit whose interests are indifferent to ours. Neither does a spirit need to love you or care for your precious life to give you boons and blessings, though there are those that do. With slow magic, we wield the scepter of our self-sovereignty while opening to the wild intuitive powers of the other-than-human worlds. We need not tolerate abuse from any spirits. Gods may bring you ordeals, but if those serve you, the trials will make you stronger and more alive. Those are experiences to revere. They should not convince you that you are garbage. If all you experience in the care of a god or spirit is misfortune, illness, distress, power-lessness, and self-hatred, that being is not your friend.

When experiencing a significant emotional reaction to a spirit, take extra care to attend to your scared or intimidated parts before proceeding. Check out their concerns and help them find safety—whether that safety is in the physical world, with magical tools, or in an imaginal realm where they can feel secure and empowered. You may learn to approach every spirit in your work with calmness, confidence, and the ease of knowing your power and self-sovereignty. Working in this state offers more safety than working out of fear, anger, or desperation. This is the merit of doing the inner work and knowing one's self while also working with spirits. We become better at sensing our patterns and all the parts of us that offer their colors and textures to the world. We separate those out from the shape and sound of what is beyond us. What I've found to be true is that when I am too emotionally charged, I'm unlikely to get accurate information. When I can get into a calm, centered state and stay curious, the truth emerges. I cannot tell you what the truth feels like, other than its apprehension makes life work better. The truth often surprises us, though once it is named, it seems obvious and clear. The truth may feel uncomfortable, inconvenient, and frustrating, but it rarely anni-hilates us. Often truth is more profound and less catastrophic than we imagine it will be. Shifting our perspective in this way lowers the tension around receiving gnosis, which makes us more relaxed and able to take in nuanced and complex information. All you need to do is show up and receive; you can decide later what to do with the information.

Spirit Talk

Reflect on the following questions: What are your assumptions about the spiritual worlds? What are your fears when it comes to listening to gods and other spirits? What are your hopes when it comes to listening to gods and other spirits? After a day, come back to your answers. Notice how the answers appear to you when you have space and perspective. Are any of your hopes and fears familiar? Do versions of them show up in the context of work, family, or relationships?

Underline the answers that resonate with you in a way that feels exciting and expansive. Draw a box around the answers that feel limiting, constricting, or disturbing. Draft a brief statement about what you'd like from spirit contact, how you are willing to grow, and what you are unwilling to sacrifice. Create sacred space and stand at your altar, and communicate this statement to the spirit world. Listen for what comes back.

Who Is Listening?

When our spirits talk to us, what we perceive may say more about ourselves in the moment than it does about the spirit. When we encounter something fearful, pathetic, aggrandizing, these may all be filtered through the emotional state we have brought to the conversation. We can explore this in this exercise, as well as get practice with moving into clear connection.

In a calm, safe place, take three deep breaths and exhale completely at the end of each. Let your eyes close or your gaze soften. Imagine there is a pathway stretching ahead of you ridged with stone markers on each side, passing through a grassy meadow into a cave nestled beneath a mountain ridge. Follow the path into the cave, letting your senses take in the darkness. As you breathe and move, imagine that ahead of you are four great torches mounted against the wall of an opening. The roof of the cave curves overhead, gathering the light. In the center stands the peacock. Surrounding the peacock are several sets of clothing and masks. Each mask has matching colored glass across the holes of the eyes, ears, and mouth. These clothes hang on racks waiting for you, and each is marked with words evoking states of being. Take time trying on each set of clothes and gazing upon the peacock. Notice how the peacock appears to you when you're in this set of clothes, through this mask, filtered through this color. Find and try on the clothes that match these states:

- Anger at the gods
- Fear of the gods
- Longing to be saved
- Seeking to be devoured
- Demanding to be exalted

For each set of clothes, notice how it feels to be wearing them and how you experience the peacock in this state. Remove and return the clothes, and notice how the peacock appears to you now before moving to the next. If you notice other sets of clothes that call to you, try those on as well and note your experience in them. Pay particular attention to the ways in which you can put on and take off each set of clothing.

God Soul

When engaging in spirit work, our greatest ally and protector is our god soul. The teaching that each of us has a personal divinity that dwells slightly overhead comes from the Anderson Feri tradition. To my best understanding, it includes influences from similar teachings in African and indigenous Hawaiian spiritual practice. Victor Anderson, progenitor of Feri with his wife Cora, made a number of claims to either having trained in certain indigenous traditions or having had access to their gnosis through being in that lineage in a previous life or initiated in this life. As I am not involved in indigenous Hawaiian or African traditional religions, I will not be using their symbols, myths, or names in this writing, but I acknowledge their influence in the legacy of magic I have received.

Our god soul is the part of us closest to the vastness of God Herself; it carries divine wisdom and the perspective of having once been immersed in the all, having experienced multiple lifetimes. If God Herself is all, she is too distant and grand to fully connect with us humans. It is akin to our difficulty in having a personal relationship with all the bacteria living in our digestive tracts. But if we were God, we could give each bacterium a piece of our essence to then experience the world as bacterium and guide each in service of our wholeness.

Imagine that God Herself is a grand bonfire and your god soul is a spark that drifted into the night and came to rest inside your body, longing to experience this material world, including mortality, limitations, and change. Yet it retains that memory of what it was like to be all, the vast perspective of God Herself. That hot spark of divinity lands uncomfortably upon the cold wet earth. We may go through our entire life unaware of god soul, or haunted by it. It is always with us, hovering slightly overhead, and we can bring it more fully into connection with all of our parts through soul alignment, regular meditation, and deep practice.[30] Knowing and honoring our god soul first offers great protection and guidance when navigating the other spiritual realms.

God soul's only agenda is to witness you, to love you, to help you be fully yourself. When encountering any other spirit, especially if it feels off, I'll send a breath up to god soul and ask for its help in discerning what's happening. So, too, can we breathe up charged emotions and confusions of any kind, asking for god soul's help in sorting through what is best for us. It is said that god soul communicates directly with our instinctive, animal soul, so after sending my confusion or desire up, I check in with my instincts and hope for the best in following them. Though we thrive when connected to god soul, we naturally fall out of alignment as part of the normal wear and tear of living in this world. Rather than scrutinizing yourself and others for signs of alignment, it's better to breathe the energy of that curiosity up for your own alignment. Daily alignment practice is like brushing your teeth. Doing so helps to maintain your good health and reduces the likelihood of problems down the road. Not doing so, however, does not need to be a moral condemnation. Even if you've forgotten for months, you can start again.

EXERCISE
Cultivating Intimacy with God Soul

Feel how your feet or your seat press down toward the ground and how the ground presses up to meet the force

---

30. My version of soul alignment is available in the "Daily Practice" section of the "Stepping Onto the Path" chapter.

of gravity. Take in that feeling of support and breathe it into your core. Imagine your center is a vessel of power and every breath fills it more to the brim. When you feel your center is almost bursting, exhale it upward, imagining that your god soul above you gathers that power into itself and then reaches down with a fiery tether to anchor itself to your core, moving your life force through your body.

Imagine opening your head like a chalice to receive the presence of your god soul. Notice how it flows into you and what it reveals to you. Open all the sensory organs in your head to receive what god soul wishes to offer. After sitting with this for a time, breathe the energy from your head and your belly into your heart. When you exhale, imagine that connection ripples out from your chest like the surface of a pond into which a stone has been dropped. Breathe with this connection and bring energy up and down, allowing it to move outward easily, naturally, in its own way.

Chapter 10

SPIRIT ALLIES OF SLOW MAGIC

The theological framework of this book honors simultaneous unity and multiplicity, which is not an uncommon spiritual framework even within monotheistic religions. God Herself is the totality. Each of us is an expression of her, and she is the ground of our being. That is the widest, broadest possible view. Moving closer to the specific reveals more and more multiplicity, diversity, and nuance. We could call upon the grandest of all deities for aid, or we could call upon a specific aspect of deity who is intimately familiar with our specific problem. I've heard practitioners question working with "smaller" gods and spirits, asking, "Why call the janitor when you could call the CEO?" But if you spill milk in the middle of a grocery store, it's not the CEO who's going to come clean it. It's useful to be friendly with many kinds of spirits for aid.

In each relationship we retain a quality of consciousness that can blend with different energies and perspectives but retain its essential nature, unharmed, when unblended. Awareness is like a mirror that can reflect multitudes without changing its nature. When spirits merge consciousnesses with each other or with us, we briefly become a different and unique experience in the world that can separate out again. The unifying consciousness of God Herself is the totality that differentiates into the experiences of duality through the twins. We could also experience the division of four cardinal elemental energies, seven planetary energies, thousands of gods, or billions of human consciousnesses. The peacock returns to totality knowing the sorrows and pleasures of disintegration. Earlier, we worked with an exercise of the flame of God Herself dividing into the twins, and then those flames reuniting as the peacock. The blending of these consciousnesses produces a being beyond its composite parts—much like how drinking blended chocolate milk is a completely different experience than drinking pure milk and eating straight chocolate, even if you do both at the same time.

Having discussed the merit of allies in the previous chapter, we will now look at different kinds of spirits: ancestors, elementals, gods, and the spirits of place.[31] This is by no means an exhaustive examination of spirits you may befriend or encounter on your journey. These particular spirits aid slow magic in their capacity to reveal and guide us in navigating the magical currents in which we do our work. Ancestors may be our greatest allies, our enduring source of support and life force, yet they hold the deeper wounds that limit our potential. Befriending gods, elementals, and the spirits of place roots us deeply into a relationship with the currents of energy. They teach us new ways to do magic and guide us in doing magic in alignment with the currents we face in the moment.

Ancestors

As I learned witchcraft, ancestor work was acknowledged and encouraged, but I was not given much guidance on the specifics of practice. Many of us had difficult relationships with our families and could not imagine much solace to be found there. Ancestors may

---

31. I use "god" as a gender-inclusive term.

have been violent and abusive, leaving deep scars that were never discussed or seemingly inescapable. Likely all of us have ancestors who did things we find repugnant and immoral. For years, my own ancestors tended to be silent when I did attempt any kind of work. Finally, there came a time when a strange spirit confronted me in the guise of a being more recognizable from Vodun, which led me to consult with a Manbo who set me on the journey I needed. Now I think the ancestral silence I mistook as exile was actually a complete absence of connection and vitality. Our ancestral lineages are like power lines that transmit energy between us and the great spirits of our families. If those lines are not tended and maintained, they become corroded and weak. The flow of power is impeded by unresolved trauma, secrets, and emotional complexes. As magical workers, we have the skills to unbind those blocks and increase the flow of vitality through the family lines.

There are spirits who love your family lines and beings of power in your heritage who you can aid and support through offerings and prayers in strengthening the connection. Even if recent ancestors do not welcome contact, there will be someone in your ancestral lineage who understands, appreciates, and honors your work. If you do not have a specific name, imagine yourself moving back, back, back, until you find a connection. Ancestor veneration has healed my relationship with my family members in ways I never could have imagined or accomplished on my own. Now I know that I belong and am deeply loved, though for a long time I had given up on feeling that way.[32] The spirits of those we knew in life have a different perspective—more expansive and flexible,

---

32. If you want to go deeper, Daniel Foor's *Ancestral Medicine* (Bear & Company, 2017) is a great resource for inspiration in this work; it is written to be accessible to any spiritual tradition or orientation.

though still comforted by the familiar images and prayers of their religions.

There is merit in working with ancestors of your family lineages whether by blood or adoption, as those are the lines through which are transmitted burdens and gifts. Repairing ancestral lines may surface family secrets and the burdens those ancestors carried. Be gentle with yourself when this happens. The truth can be deeply shocking and alter your understanding of your family and your own story. Yet there is freedom in knowing the hard stuff. We learn to see our parents and ancestors in their full humanity, capable of beauty and harm, allowing us more of our own humanity. Their stories of survival and ups and downs may entertain, inspire, or warn. Suddenly our own sufferings feel less personal. Many problems in life that we think are "only mine" are rooted deeply in the family tree; old stories trying to work themselves out across the generations. Our parents had to cope with this legacy and tried to teach us what helped them survive. These solutions may not be right for us and may have harmed us. We can both name the harm and honor the love.

As our story of the past changes, we are freed to envision new futures with the aid of those who love and care for us. Ancestor work need not be about forgiving and forgetting. Some cultures with strong ancestor practices do work to bind those who were criminal or violent in life to the work of protecting others from those harms in death. Those who are hostile to us need not be welcome at our altars, though they may have to learn to get past their biases if you're the only living descendant available to support them. Should you decide to give offerings and prayers for the uplift and empowerment of your ancestral line, you can make clear in your prayers and magic that those violent and uncouth ancestors must work to repair their legacies if they wish to be welcome at your altar. Witches and magic workers whose relationships with birth family are too fraught may choose to prioritize ancestors more personally meaningful, like chosen ancestors, ancestors of the craft, ancestors of their identity, community ancestors, and so forth. If this calls to you, it helps with building confidence in yourself and your work.

My practice is to have a permanent altar with symbols of my maternal and paternal grandparents, along with a place of honor for my queer ancestors of blood and cultural lineage. I honor the ancestors of my spiritual tradition and the ancestors of the place upon which I live—those generations of my country who have lived on this land, and those peoples who have lived here and known the land before European settlers arrived. Once a week, I leave offerings of clean water, incense, food, a lit candle, and prayers for the uplift and strengthening of my ancestral lineages, going back to those in my line who are the most healed and in their power. The prayers I offer for my ancestors' healing and uplift come from their religious tradition—the Our Father and Hail Mary—rather than from my own. If there are foods, drinks, or prayers they would like and recognize, I prioritize those.

EXERCISE
Work with Ancestors

Set aside a space where you can put pictures, images, or treasures associated with your family lines. You can represent the lineages meaningful to you—biological parents and grandparents; adoptive parents; friends who are family; ancestors of your spiritual practice; cultural ancestors; heroic ancestors; ancestors of the place in which you live. I'd recommend starting simple, however. Start leaving regular offerings, weekly or monthly. A glass of clean water is a good minimum, but if there's particular kinds of foods or treats they'd like (that won't get eaten by pets, pests, or small children) you could leave those as well. When you do, take a moment to imagine all the way back in that lineage to a person filled with all the power and vitality of your line. I call them the "great grand-ancestors." Invite them to connect with you through your lines and ask what they need from you.

Guardians and Beasts

The guardians connect to the primal forces of reality, akin to the mythical creatures of spirit who elude our human categories. These spirits are like gods yet show up as strange, alien, or vast. The difference is like talking to a tsunami rather than a local natural spring. When we want to explore territory beyond the fence line demarcating what we know, they escort us far afield into the unknowable. When we turn toward them, call their names, and connect, new gifts and revelations come. They are like tuning forks emitting a pure frequency, inviting us to resonate with their vibration. If unmediated, their force could overwhelm us. Approaching with respect and humility invites their kindness in stepping down the intensity of force to what we can tolerate.

In Morningstar, we have names for the elemental guardians both within our school and inherited from the Anderson Feri tradition.[33] My sense is that the names we use are a glimmer of light across a vast surface. There is a guardian for each cardinal direction as well as the spaciousness above, the gravity below, and the center in which we live. They align with conventional associations of

---

33. I do not think the names of these beings are necessary for you in developing your own relationship, but one set of names is published in T. Thorn Coyle's *Evolutionary Witchcraft* (Weiser Books, 2004).

elemental correspondence, with east governing air, south governing fire, west governing water, and north governing earth. Above, below, and center belong to the column of spirit. Occasionally I dedicate a month to each of these beings. In the morning I get up, do my regular practice, turn in the direction of the guardian, intone its name while sending out my desire to connect, and then wait for how they show up. The practice has deepened my relationship with the elemental domains of the guardians, but each time has also surprised me with new insights, tools, and practices. The first time through, the guardian of the east would pierce my heart with their crystal-tipped wand; the guardian of the south pierced my belly with their blade; the guardian of the west planted their chalice in my skull. Some of these associations made sense while others surprised me, and these images were insistent and nothing I'd otherwise anticipated would happen. As a result of working with these energy centers in my body and these implicit correspondences, much has since evolved in my practice. The second time I did this working, the guardians gave me recipes for ritual baths and sprays, as well as homework that I strongly disliked, but they also offered important gifts.

Beasts are the creatures depicted in myth who draw fascination: gorgons, chimeras, manticores, sirens, dragons, and more. They are less grand and overwhelming than guardians, and yet I find them to trouble the boundary between the human and greater-than-human worlds. In a sense, beasts embody mysteries at the margins of human civilization that we may not wish to face, but their gifts may be ones we need. During the #MeToo era, when women and others spoke out against the sexual violence they experienced, I and other witches sensed the presence of Medusa, a gorgon who was transformed into a beast after experiencing sexual violence from Poseidon in the temple of Athena. Medusa's story evokes the layers of victimization that happen with sexual assault—first the harm itself, then the blaming and exile of the victim along with the protection of the powerful perpetrator. Feminist tellings of this story suggest Medusa's transformation was a protective gift to ward off would-be predators with a glare that turns them to stone.

My sense is that both guardians and beasts have an interest in the development of humanity and a willingness to participate in our evolution, but to what end, I am unsure. They seem not to care for worship or reverence, nor ask for offerings. The scale of their concerns may be vast and hard to comprehend, but they seem to need those of us willing to become more conscious of their powers and skills. Working with these beings helps us to both orient our magic in time and space and align it with the great elemental currents within their care.

EXERCISE
Connecting to the Guardians

This practice seems simple but becomes profound if you persist. We find these beings at the furthest edges of the cosmos and in the extremes of the four cardinal directions and the above, below, and center. Dedicate at least a week to each of the directions. Every day, for a few minutes, turn your body or attention toward that direction. Meditate on the elemental associations you have with this direction. Send your breath toward the furthest edge of what is possible in this direction. Ask the spirit of this element to show you a form that you are ready to perceive. Wait, and notice what happens. See if a name comes to you, or a vision, or a sensation. Work with what is given.

EXERCISE
Befriending a Beast

If there is a mythical creature that intrigues you, take a little time to read about the mythology associated with it—ancient sources if they're available, contemporary ones if they exist. Notice shared attributes among these depictions and differences. When you feel calm and know you'll be uninterrupted, take time to go into trance. Slow your breathing down and let your body move the way it wants to move. Hum and sway. Start to imagine a trail, and follow it. As you follow this path, notice what senses feel sharp and what feels dull or absent. Stay with what you know—the feeling of the path moving beneath you, the sound of movement, the sight of the trail curving around a bend.

Imagine this path leads you up a green, grassy hill that looks out over a beautiful view. You can see an ocean, a river, a mountain, a valley with deep caves, a place of ancient ruins, a desert. Your perception is vast and extends in so many directions, taking in possibilities. In this place, call to that beast that intrigues you: gorgon, minotaur, manticore, unicorn, jackalope, dragon, siren. Chimeras or aliens. Whichever it is, invite it to come to you, or notice if you need to move toward it. Whether it comes to you or you move close, make sure you are in a safe space and observe this beast from a distance. Do not rush toward it or run away from it. Know that it cannot hurt you in this trance. Ask it to show itself to you. Ask it the questions you have. Ask for a blessing or a story. See what comes up.

Gods

Like the guardians, gods are closely intertwined with the forces governing our lives, but they tend to be more differentiated and closer to humans in perspective, which makes them both easier and trickier to engage. Some precede agriculture and have little interest in our contemporary ways, whereas others are involved in human culture and civilization, spurring the revolutions of new technology, maintaining systems of law and justice, or aligning with the dispossessed and marginalized. Whether gods are stories, personifications of psychological forces, or real consciousnesses with their own agency, they are potent, deep, complex, and conscious, appearing in unexpected ways. Our relationships to gods may be as child to parent, lover to lover, or protector to vulnerable creature, with deep awe and reverence, playful mirth, or rage and resentment. I experience the gods as great enough that they can handle any feeling we have toward them. Harsh feelings reflect importance as much as warmth; it is indifference that separates them from us.

In our relationships with gods, contracts matter. I do not mean a legalistic document of prescribed behaviors—though such an arrangement may be useful if the deity's contact is disruptive to your life. But *contract* here encompasses a softer, broader sense of the agreements and shape of relationship. Is this a god whom I am asking for one favor, who requires a service from me? Is this a god with whom I relate in deep filial love and devotion? Do my gods like for me to follow prescribed rituals or speak spontaneously from the heart? We have the right to negotiate what is asked of us. We have the right to set limits and declare what is not possible for us. We have the right to tell the gods what we need from them to do what's being asked. We have the right to refuse, though saying no may have unwanted consequences. Try not to feel a sense of doom when reading that; it is true any relationship. If someone wants to be your lover but you only want to be their friend, they may be unable to meet you and choose instead to give up the relationship entirely. There are times when clarity lets you find a relationship that works for you both, but if that's not possible, it's better for the relationship to end than for either party to pretend to be what the other wants. Dignity and self-respect are worth the cost.

There are practitioners who speak of god relationships in which personal agency is limited to nonexistent. They can't say no, and they must find a way to work with what is being demanded of them. I've yet to experience this kind of dominance but acknowledge this as their truth. If you find yourself in this kind of relationship and it distresses you, I would encourage you to turn toward your god soul and your ancestors to ask for discernment and advice. Check in with yourself and see if parts of you are feeling helpless, small, overwhelmed, or consumed by the god. Then see if you can step out of those parts and offer them support. If after all this, you still experience that lack of agency and it's a relationship you want to continue, I encourage you to continue to seek help from your community until you find a mentor who can support you.

The Souls of the World and of Place

The soul of the world, or *anima mundi*, is the local spirit of our planet. It comprises the awareness of all living beings and is its own intelligence that influences and guides the development of life for those who listen. As God Herself is all things and her own thing, so the soul of the world is of the earth itself. This soul speaks to us through dreams, trance, inspiration, and vision. When we feel a general unsettledness that is collective yet undefined, we itch with a drive coming from this soul. The soul of the world is like the mycorrhizal network that connects the roots of trees in a forest together, along which information and resources are shared to those far apart, occasionally bursting from the ground with a mushroom head. Those of us who listen calmly with curiosity and attend to our dreams and visions have a particular receptivity to the soul's guidance.

When revolutionary ideas and forms emerge, driving forward evolution and the functioning of life on earth, they are driven by this soul. We can see this phenomenon when similar ideas and forms appear spontaneously in multiple places. Convergent evolution is the tendency of different species to evolve similar traits though they have small genetic relationships with each other. One such tendency, when unrelated crustaceans evolve into the shape of crabs, has its own name: *carcinisation*. We can also see this in human cultures when certain ideas, certain kinds of ritual or medicine, certain stories emerge in vastly different contexts without any apparent exchange. I've experienced this myself, when I decided to write a book-length work on the Iron Pentacle, a tool that until then had only been shared orally and written about in essays and chapters. Yet as I was in the process of finishing and preparing to publish mine, lo and behold, I learned that my colleagues Jane Meredith and Fio Gede Parma were publishing their own book-length work on the same practice.

As God Herself is the larger being who contains the soul of the world, so too does the soul of the world contain the multiplicity of local spirits of place. Smaller, more local spirits are nested within the larger, but those spirits have more specificity and concrete help to offer within their domain. God Herself would say, "All is love, and you are all my children." The spirit of your neighborhood might say, "That's a good place to plant a shrub." Both are valuable, but one is more practical. Spirits of place want us to be embedded in them, to listen to and honor them. When we eat food and drink water from the place in which we reside, we take the spirit of the place into us. When we bury our dead, nurture our lands, and celebrate with neighbors, we invest ourselves into the spirit of our place.

EXERCISE
Connecting to the Spirits of Place

Get paper and a pen or an audio recorder to document what arises. Close your eyes, or soften your gaze, and focus on exhaling slowly and completely until you are empty. Let yourself rest empty for a moment, then inhale, and then focus on exhaling slowly and completely again. With every exhalation, see if you can get a little slower, a little more empty each time. Let the inhales take care of themselves. Notice whatever is present for you, and ask these thoughts and feelings if they could give you space. Do not worry about emptying your mind or coming to full silence. Ask for space.

Now imagine sending out a greeting to the room you are in. You could speak with words or with the warmth of your heart. Connect to the spirit of this room. "Hi, Room, I'd like to learn more about you. What do you want to share with me?" Breathe, and pay attention. You might have sensations in your body, emotions, memories, thoughts, or energy fluctuations. You might notice things in your environment in a particular way or feel how you are in the space differently. Hold all of these as communications from the spirit in the room.

Thank the spirit, and breathe your awareness bigger. Imagine the entire building in which you are. Send out your curiosity to connect to the spirit of this building. Notice what changes in your awareness, what information comes. Thank this spirit, and breathe your awareness bigger. Ask to connect with the Spirit of the Place in which you currently are. Imagine the breadth and depth of this place—the buildings and roads surrounding you, the plants and animals with you, the landscapes of mountain or river, forest or sand. Notice how you imagine the limits of the spirit of this place—don't get hung up on being too precise.

Thank this spirit and breathe your awareness bigger. Ask to connect with the *anima mundi*, the soul of the world. Drop your awareness deep into the earth and broaden it across the surface of the planet until your sense encompasses the entire globe. Listen, sense, and receive what it wants to share with you. Thank this spirit, and imagine you can breathe yourself bigger. Ask to connect to God Herself. Dwell within the totality of her being and see what is offered to you.

Find your connection to the earth. Notice the edges of your body and the feeling of how it sits, stands, or lies in the room you are in. Let your awareness inhabit your body fully, and sit up. You are God Herself, and you are yourself. Take a moment to ground yourself by remembering who you are: say your name and touch the edges of your body. If you are struggling, press gently into the top of your head and soles of your feet, imagining you can close these energy centers. Drinking water is also a great way to ground.

Ending a Bad Relationship

The guideline of being a good houseguest with spirits applies in relationships where you are receiving good hospitality. If we behave with humility, respect, and care, we have a right to expect to be treated with support, concern, and connection. If we feel endangered or harmed by the relationship, we have the right to protect ourselves. Spirits can lie and misrepresent their intentions and who they are, and even relationships with well-intentioned spirits may end up bad for us. If you are unsure if you are in a bad relationship, the first step is to engage in discernment. Talk to people you trust about what is going on and your questions and concerns, and get their feedback. If you know good diviners, priests, or spirit-sensitive people, get their opinion. Do your own research on the spirit, if you can, to get a sense if what's happening is in alignment with other reports of work with this being. Breathe energy to your god soul and ask it for clarity about the situation.

If you need to set limits, get clear on what's not working for you. Make or create an image of the spirit. Grab the tool that shows your power—a wand, athame, other objects or symbols—and cast a circle. Call the spirit into the image and tell it firmly what is no longer working for you. If you are open to negotiation, ask the spirit what else could make your relationship work. Or you can tell the spirit to go find a place where it will be welcome. If you do this, take the image of the spirit physically outside the edges of what you would consider your home and leave it there. Afterward, take a bath with Epsom salts. Bless the water with a prayer to a beloved god or protective spirit, and ask the water to cleanse your energy bodies of all that is drawing this unwanted attention.

Cleanse your house in your preferred way. I have a stick of dried lavender and rosemary from my garden that I use to do a smoke cleanse. You could mix up a solution of salt water and bless it with a prayer to God Herself for help in dispelling any malignant, toxic, or chaotic energies that do not serve your magic. Walk around your place flicking the water, if that feels appropriate. Open your windows to help clear these energies with a natural breeze. Use your wand or athame and surround your house with golden light or protective flame or energetic brambles, asking the boundary to keep out what is unwholesome to you and allow in what serves and loves you. In most cases, regular spiritual cleansing of your body, souls, and dwelling will be enough to shed malignant forces. Having a good relationship with your god soul, ancestors, and other beneficent spirits adds more protection and support. If all else fails, there is more to try.

EXERCISE
The Nuclear Option

If you are bothered by a spirit and none of these suggestions have helped, here is a spell of last resort. Make a poppet to represent yourself. Create sacred space. Imagine what within you that is attracting the spirit's attention. Imagine that you can take that out of you, put it inside the poppet, and seal it inside. Ask this poppet-part of you if it knows what about it fascinates the spirit. Ask if there is any way to transform this part of you to stop being bothered. If there is a possibility of transformation, follow that guidance instead of completing this ritual. If there is no actionable information, or you tried the guidance and it failed but you are resolved to be free of the spirit's bothering, take a blade and use it to cut any spiritual cords that connect you to the energy that is now in the poppet. Once the poppet contains this energy and is disconnected from you, offer it to the spirit in your stead. Call the poppet by your name and tell the spirit this now belongs to it. Go leave the poppet in a place sacred to the spirit or god— if there's no obvious answer, leave it at a crossroads—and walk away without looking back. Later, call upon beloved spirits and ask for their aid in filling the space of what you've lost with energy that supports you.

Chapter 11

THE COMPASS OF COMMUNITY

In the work of slow magic, we can do nothing without affecting others, whether casting a spell in our own rooms or raising energy with a throng of dancing witches. There is a difference, however, between the magic we do in solitude and what we do in community. Sharing ritual and magic brings life, passion, and depth that is difficult to access on our own. With trust, we can relax our guarded parts and loose the wildness of our magical nature. When run by a skilled facilitator, my trances are far more deep and profound than what I can access by myself. No ritual is as intense and gratifying as one shared with those who show up with sincere engagement.

There is a complementary relationship between community and personal ritual that establishes its own upwards spiral. The discipline of daily practices improves our focus, efficacy in running energy, sensitivity, and gravity of center that helps us show up and stay present. We become a blade that is ever-sharper and more precise, and we add its potency to the workings of the group. In turn, community ritual catalyzes magical work, offers witness to ongoing transformation, and gives a framework to make sense of our experiences. The more you engage with the cosmology and lore of your group—its gods, spirits, and mythos—the more alive it becomes.

A living tradition is itself an accomplishment of slow magic. Magical work and spirit relationships weave into cultural norms and traditions that get passed from one generation to the next to create a lineage. The lineage is a soul unto itself, guiding the group's work and initiating change in its membership. Living tradition sustains magic in the world, like a flame passed from candle to candle, remaining essentially itself though it is in constant transformation. The tradition's norms and cosmology make your inner world intelligible to yourself and your peers, teachers, and elders in your community. With this shared language, you can aid each other with discernment. If you were to come to me and say, "I had a vision of the peacock. He told me I was a worthless piece of trash," I would ask us to pause. "That doesn't sound like the peacock to me," I'd respond. "Let's look at what else might be happening."

As one who has spent most of my adult life building or in leadership of communities, I'm a believer in their power and potency. I also deeply empathize with those who mistrust community. Adding more people multiplies the complexities of politics. I've learned through bad examples, I've learned through good examples, and I've learned that some patterns tend to arise seemingly no matter what one does. In my most idealistic and utopian visions, I imagine a community of shared religion where we live in deep relationship with the land, sharing resources, meeting together to work through conflicts and harms, engaging in regular ritual to connect ourselves to our gods and each other. My heart hurts with how tenuous this vision feels. I've known Pagan communities and land projects that did amazing work and ultimately dissolved due to economic problems and community conflict. I bow in amazement to those groups who maintain their continuity for decades. Yet I must also honor the powerful choice of dissolving a group when its work is done. Witches and Pagans tend to be cantankerous and enamored of the sovereignty of the individual, chafing at the bullying, guilting, or other coercions that would keep a long-term community in existence. That does not mean we are immune to manipulation and coercion, but we seem more at peace with dissolution as an acceptable outcome when a group has served its purpose.

This chapter is about the merits of working in groups and offers a framework for those thinking about building a group or wanting to assess their group. There are legal and logistical questions that arise when groups commit to tasks such as becoming a nonprofit, which are better discussed with a lawyer, if that is your path. What I want to focus on is the spirit that motivates these actions, using the image of a compass. We can form a simple analog compass with a circle, a center, and a needle. All three together give us orientation. In groups, the circle demarcates the group's membership and responsibilities. The center indicates the leadership and governance of the group. The needle points toward the group's mission and purpose. As we will see, the three are interdependent—pulling them apart shows how much they define each other—and separating them out allows us to better observe the whole.

Circle

The circle establishes the boundaries and terrain of the community. Within the circle are the members, constituents, and stakeholders of the group. Outside of the circle are other people. The responsibility of the group extends through the interior of the circle and ends at its edges. What is outside the circle still matters, of course, and the group may take a role in the dealings and concerns of the larger world. But what is within the circle has greater weight, import, and immediacy to the group. There can be circles within the circle. Some groups have an inner circle that separates out the more casual membership from those deeply committed to learning and tending its mysteries. Other groups have circles for sub-groups, like committees to focus on particular tasks and projects.

Let me speak to my passion about a clearly drawn circle: my first witchcraft community aspired to inclusive, non-hierarchical organization. Anyone who showed up to meetings or rituals, or who agreed with a statement of principle that unified us, had an opinion that mattered in our decision-making and planning process. We had no definition of membership beyond whomever showed up, and no way to track who considered themselves members. As a young Aries leaving a hierarchical religion of origin, I found this approach liberating and empowering. As I stepped into greater leadership, however, I found this structure incredibly frustrating and demoralizing. Any decision we made could be thrown into question and undone by the criticisms of people who weren't at the meetings. People who never came to meetings or rituals nevertheless criticized our decisions from the edges, writing screeds on our mailing lists about how we were doing it wrong. Occasionally a person would get involved and make declarations that our organization was "hated" by "a lot of people" in community that we needed to win over. We didn't get names of these people or specifics on what they hated. Claiming to speak for an anonymous horde of angry people had a double effect of inflating this person's opinions while making it impossible to respond. How do you engage with vague criticism? How could we know this horde even existed? What if it was one or two annoyed people who moved on with their lives?

Those particular kinds of comments broke my enthusiasm for ambiguous structure. I couldn't worry about the opinions of people who didn't show up or engage openly with their problems. Those people, of course, do matter, and their concerns could be completely valid, but it's impossible to work through conflicts with those who are not participating. The accelerated path to leadership burn-out looks like second-guessing every decision with anxiety about alienating a nebulous group of people. Then you start doing things like holding off on making decisions at meetings until you send a poll to the people who didn't show up, to make sure that they feel included in the process. In my experience, the people who don't come to meetings rarely respond to polls. You end up learning nothing and still feel hesitant to move forward with a decision. Having a clear circle matters for the functioning and well-being of a community. The opinions and needs of your membership necessarily bear greater weight than the opinions of strangers. Knowing who is in your circle helps you know to do outreach and check in when someone goes quiet and distant, rather than wondering if they're coming back. Having a defined circle requires clearly marked gates for entry and exit. "Gatekeeping" is a contentious word that has connotations of elitism and unfair discrimination, which are absolutely risks in this kind of boundary-making. Yet we still need gates to know who is in and out of the circle, and we need keepers to guard against unwanted intrusions and unacknowledged departures.

Entering a circle involves consenting, to a certain extent, to the circle's norms, beliefs, and practices. If you want to be a part of the group, you need to know the expectations for how they practice. You need to learn their customs and ways and make them your own. Going through a mystery school, a course of training, an apprenticeship toward initiation changes the conditions of your soil to be more favorable to the growth of those seeds of mystery. Less esoterically, every group has a culture of its own, including in-jokes, ways of dealing with (or avoiding) conflict, decision-making, and conducting ritual. It's normal to feel ambivalent about these customs. If you want to change the group, it's more effective when doing so from a place of deep love, appreciation, and understanding of its ways. There is a place for critiquing groups and seeing opportunities to help it grow. But if you find you have no appreciation whatsoever for how a group works, that's a good reason not to join. There are other groups out there; no one of them possesses all the secrets of magic and the gods. You also have the option to draw your own circle and build a group better aligned with your interests.

Center

When a circle forms, a center emerges. The center brings coherence to the circle. In witchcraft rituals, we tend to form a circle of participants. Ritualists step into the center to connect with participants and to be seen and heard most clearly. They step into the center to do their work and then rejoin the circle. We also place altars at the center, giving dwelling to the gods, spirits, or symbols that serve as the center of gravity for the community. Every point in a circle is equidistant from the center. From the center, you can therefore see and be seen by those in the circle equally. You can take in the entire circle, whereas those at the edges struggle to see what's happening on the other side. The burden, opportunity, and responsibility of being in the center is this state of being connected to, and yet separate from, the circle.

What happens at the center affects the entire circle. Here lies both the human governance and spiritual core of the group. A charismatic leader might live here, holding the group together through the members' admiration and longing for proximity. In other groups, an established legacy of teachings and practice is at the center, passed from generation to generation. Often there is tension between the center and the circle because of their relationship of interdependence and distance. As much as the center sees the whole, the perspective at the edge of the circle is much different. Those at the center might feel exhausted and overworked, begging for more engagement, while those at the edges see exclusion and power-tripping. It is easy to see this as a conflict of individual personalities, but it is intriguing to watch what happens when people move from edge to center and center to edge. The person who was once the outspoken rebel tends to start sounding like the leaders they critiqued.

The center must act in the interests of the whole, while those at the edges emphasize their specific position. Being in the center infuses you with the group's power, which makes your words and actions have greater impact. You may not feel powerful at first; indeed, those new to the center feel much the same as they did at the edge. But they'll see the effects of this power in how others respond to them—with obsequiousness, with rebellion, with hurt and upset, with unsettling compliance. Two peers can give each other hard feedback, but a teacher or council leader giving the same feedback could bruise, or crumble, or draw out an aggressive response. Those at the center must learn to wield their power with softness and responsibility.

Needle

The needle of a compass always points north, helping us to orient ourselves whenever we're lost. Even if we're not going north, knowing where it is helps us to find where we're headed. In the work of groups, the needle points toward the group's mission. It's the guiding purpose and function to which the group can return whenever things get too complex. It is normal for people to come to groups with all manner of different needs, dreams, and desires, as well as a willingness to fight to make the group fulfill everything. But a group needs a specific task for which it exists, otherwise all the energy that could go toward collaborative work instead becomes ensnarled by interpersonal conflict and power games.

Here is the slow magic: the needle as the will of a group, directing us toward clear and achievable intention. An example of a group's mission could be, "Meeting the spiritual needs of our membership through the practice of witchcraft." That would make having regular full moon rituals within their tradition part of the primary mission. As the group grows in comfort and strength, it may take on other tasks like meeting social needs, mutual aid for members, political activism, charitable works, or running big public events to bring others together. Yet if any of these tasks eclipse the primary mission of the group, things get weird. One person's hurt feelings becomes a problem for everyone. Another person attempts an ideological coup to change the mission entirely. It's normal to have long meetings that go nowhere, or fights over who should sleep in the snoring cabin and who consistently forgets about whose gluten sensitivity. These conversations matter. They build a foundation of trust that the group can deal with conflict and work through hard problems together. But when these conversations mire us and we forget the needle, it's easy to start to wonder why we're sacrificing weekends and evenings to have the same fights we could be having with relatives.

We can assemble working compasses that last for generations or for one ritual. The merit of a compass is that it allows for greater ambition and more energy moving toward the direction of the needle. We can organize groups to do magic on behalf of our own projects, and we can marry our will to the will of a group whose magic is attempting to actualize or sustain a change in the world.

EXERCISE
Assembling a Compass

The most success I've had in organizing rituals, retreats, workshops, and so forth begins with a clear vision of what

I want so I can communicate it to others. Without the clear vision, either there's lack of engagement and enthusiasm, no follow-through, or an opportunity for others who are more decisive to take the work in a different direction. To be clear, I love collaboration and the excitement of a group coming up with ideas I wouldn't have imagined on my own. I do not love when a mission that excites me suddenly becomes irrelevant to the work of the group. This exercise is a thought experiment for starting your own compass. Once it is complete, consider trying it out.

Take a piece of paper and draw a big circle with a needle starting from the center and pointing toward a blank margin at the top of the page. Start by setting the needle of this project: What feels like an exciting, ambitious goal you want to accomplish? Along with this, consider how would you like a group to serve this goal. Would you want volunteers to organize a public ritual? Colleagues to start a coven? Community members to establish a network of mutual support? Friends to throw a themed party? You can start with the intention and then pick the structure, or vice versa. Use the work in chapter 3 to create a statement of intention for this goal. Write this statement at the top of the paper, where the needle points.

Now look to the edges of the circle. Who would you want to include in this project? Are there specific people you would invite? Are there communities you would reach out to for interest? Write those names inside the circle. Also consider—is there anyone you do *not* want involved? Write those names outside the circle. Think about the process by which you would invite and include people in the circle, and disinvite or exclude people from the circle. Write a few notes at the bottom of the page. For example: depending on the type of project, only people you invite are included, or those your closest friends have checked out and trust to participate. Another process would be to interview candidates or review applications to join the circle.

Now go to the center. Who will be in charge? How will decisions be made and communicated to the group? Do you want to do it yourself? Do you want a small team acting by consensus? Do you want the group as a whole to make proposals and vote? Are there important gods, spirits, or others who need to be consulted for the work? Write your notes here in the center.

You now have a basic framework of a proposal for a group. It's also a seed, in our frame of spellwork. As you sit with this more and begin to invite and include people, this proposal will change as it begins to sprout and grow toward flowering. If you are excited by this project and want to explore it, I recommend making a copy of the information relevant for you to remember and then using this original drawing for spellwork. If it's friendly to your ecosystem, fold the paper and bury it in a place where things grow.

Where the Compass Can Lead You

Slow magic with a group happens both for your personal work and for the larger mission of the group. As spiritual, religious, and magical groups deepen and mature, they tend to form commitments toward an ongoing project in concert with the spirits and ancestors of their lineage. Imagine the slow magic as being the work of helping those spirits retain a foothold and influence in this world. Examples of lineage-based needles include: safeguarding the sanctity of the gods, acting as a bulwark against the destroyers of consciousness, awakening humans into new ways of being, the liberation of all beings, and other grand ambitions.

The extent to which we bring the group's needle into our personal work enhances our connection. Once again we find another way in which our individual current of will becomes braided to a larger current that strengthens both. This is not to say that your entire life becomes about the needle of the group; rather, your success and the group's success becomes a mutually beneficial arrangement. Your own happiness, wellness, connection, and stability become another resource for your community; it keeps you from burning out and tests the principles of the group against what is livable in the world as it is today. It lets the soul of your community continue to learn, grow, and adapt to the changing world.

When working in relationships, it is important to be mindful of both the "I" and the "we." So often we conflate or mistake the two in ways that confuse both. I've experienced people speaking for "we" when they're putting out their own agenda and haven't checked if everyone else is on board. I've experienced putting the "we" ahead of me and forgetting that I am an integral part of the "we." There are my needs, and there are our needs. The "I" speaks for what is within the sphere of my human being—my will and desires, my dreams and reactions, my personal needs. The "we" speaks for what is within the sphere of relationships between us— our collective decisions, our identified needs, that which is necessary to keep us in harmony and together. We all need to speak first as an "I" so that we can find the consensus story of "we."

EXERCISE
The I and the We

In a sense, this exercise is the interpersonal variant of "Calling the Council" from our inner parts work. It is a simple practice to try in building relationships with members of a group, or clarifying a conflict.

First the group decides on a topic or issue to work. This need not be contentious. It could be about setting the needle of a ritual or project. Everyone meets at a scheduled time knowing that this will be the agenda of the work—don't spring this on people without the chance to prepare.

One person will need to be the facilitator, to hold the container. That person will first speak for the "we" as best as they can. Before the gathering, they should prepare a statement of the work of the group with as much clarity as possible, checking the biases that inform how they are naming the problem. An ideal statement identifies the problem afflicting the group as a whole rather than making one person or faction wrong and another right. It's not "We can't have a good potluck because of Jerry's food allergies." It's more "We're struggling to create a potluck menu that respects the energy and food needs of the group."

It won't be perfect. But start with a statement: "We are here because..." As an example: "We are gathered to set an intention for our winter solstice ritual," or "We are divided over the relationship between a teacher and a student."

Each person then has a turn to speak for their perspective on the matter. They can speak of their own stories, desires, fears, experiences, and sensations, but they should be discouraged from making accusations or assumptions of others. For example, "I feel unwanted in this group" is a personal experience that can be spoken for, whereas "Jerry is trying to get me to leave" is an accusation that imparts motives upon others that cannot be directly observed. It is easier to hear the former than the latter. Of course, if Jerry explicitly said he wants the person to leave, it can be stated as an observation. "I heard Jerry tell me he's going to do whatever he can to make me leave."

Depending upon how big the group is, consider setting time limits for each person's statement. The facilitator can also encourage people to speak of their own experience and distill what they want to say into one or two statements instead of getting lost in telling stories. Once that person has finished speaking their piece, others can ask clarifying questions to understand the speaker's perspective, but the facilitator should discourage argument, analysis, or other discussion. Instead, the goal is to make sure each person feels their perspective is understood and considered. Once that is accomplished, the speaker's turn is ended, and the next person in the circle speaks. It continues like this until everyone has had a chance to speak and be understood. The facilitator then attempts to gather the disparate experiences into a statement that names what is happening for the group. If any person feels their perspective has been erased, diminished, or vilified in the "we" statement, they can name that, and the facilitator can attempt to create a statement that best represents the entire group. After this process, it is good to take a break before moving on to generating solutions and next steps.

Meaning in Connection

When our self-esteem founders in the icy waters of life, the presence and witnessing of trusted peers and mentors sets us upright, dries us out, and pushes us forward again. As much as we are the ones who know ourselves best, the perspective of others can draw out illuminating, shocking, important truths. However, even here discernment is wise, as we know others can see us through their own fears and wounds that distort their image of who we are. We can learn to hold the observations others make of us as lightly as any prophecy or divination: take in the sliver of truth that feels valid, dismiss what seems destructive, and hold with curiosity what is still a mystery.

When we go through life, all we know is our own experience. I can never know what it's like to be in a room without me in it. My thoughts and words are so obvious to me, so normal and apparent—I live with them every second of the day—that they seem mundane and uninspired. I don't know what it's like to be hugged by my own arms, to shake my own hand, to be thrown by my own aikido. I can only learn about these through how others experience and respond. Whether people find my thoughts interesting, my jokes funny, my interjections painfully awkward—all of these tell me a bit more about myself. But it's not all about me. They also tell me about the other person's humor, interests, and connections. But it's *also* not all about them. These responses tell me and the other person about the relationship we're having in this moment. I could tell the same joke to the same person and it could result in laughter, irritation, or offense depending upon what's going on between and around us.

It's therefore useful to be open to feedback but not too precious about it. The other important truth is that diversity brings strength and resilience to a group. As a disease could wipe out an entire farm that grows a single crop, so too do groups falter when they rigidly insist on one way of being without any tolerance for other approaches. I once worked for a counseling agency that focused on a particular marginalized population, and we clinicians were passionate about advocacy for our clients' needs. Our staff meetings were feisty and combative. As a person who tends to see multiple sides to issues and likes to bring conflict to harmony, I would speak up to call out a perspective we were missing, and I also would speak up to bring the temperature down so we could hear each other better. One of my other colleagues astounded and intimidated me with their advocacy. They spoke with moral clarity and seemed unflinching in calling out problems and injustices. I honestly assumed they found me obnoxious. After one contentious meeting with an insurance agency in which I was as pissed off as everyone else, I waited much longer to step up and be the peace-maker, and my colleague noticed. They came up to me after the meeting to ask about it. They confessed that they appreciated when I took the role of mediator and depended on me to do it—though they were glad I'd waited. The communities I love best allow every-one to be themselves and flourish in the gifts that they bring. Chal-lenge is about fostering the growth of your own skills rather than demanding you become more like me. The following exercise offers a way of practicing this kind of witnessing and giving feedback.

EXERCISE
Silver and Black Mirrors

The silver mirror reflects back exactly what it sees, while the black mirror reflects a dimmed and distorted image. Witches and magicians use the black mirror to perceive occluded realities and communicate with beings in other realms. Here we will use these mirrors as another facet of the divine twins in community's capacity to witness us and help us to know ourselves more deeply.

For this, you will want a group of at least three people. Each will take a turn in every role. Larger groups can be divided in threes. If you must have a group of four or five, then everyone will take at least one turn as a quiet observer.

For the primary triad, you will have a speaker, a silver mirror, and a black mirror. The speaker will name what it is that they want to have witnessed and affirmed in community. I would recommend making a declaration of intention or sharing an issue on which you are seeking clarity.

While the speaker is making their statement, the silver mirror is watching and attending to what they perceive with their physical senses—what words are used, how the speaker moves in their body, the tone of their communication. The black mirror watches and attends to what they perceive with their inner and psychic senses—how it feels to hear the speaker, what images arise within them, what energies or symbols they perceive.

Once the speaker is done, the silver mirror reflects back what they perceived. The silver mirror should avoid editorializing or making commentary. Try to use the exact words and movements and imitation of tone to show the speaker what you witnessed.

Then the black mirror reflects back what they perceived. Again, they avoid editorializing or making commentary on the speaker, instead focusing on what they noticed within themself as they were witnessing the speaker.

The speaker takes this in for a moment. When things feel complete, the roles rotate. I would recommend the last speaker becoming the new silver mirror; the last silver mirror becoming the new black mirror; and the black mirror becoming the new speaker. If you have an observer role, I would add that into the rotation after the black mirror: the last black mirror becomes the observer, and the last observer becomes the new speaker.

Chapter 12

ADVERSITIES

I once had an artistic mobile that I hung from my ceiling; it was perfectly balanced with different shapes and colors that would rotate and shift as air circulated in the room. Should I have cut one of the shapes off, the balance would be gone and the mobile would hang in a limp mess. If I added weight to any piece of it, I'd similarly throw off the balance and disrupt the harmony of the piece. Balance is not a static state that we set and forget—it is dynamic engagement with constantly shifting forces. Changing any quality in a system affects the whole. "Good" changes can destabilize—getting a new puppy means the balance must lean hard on training and building a relationship, leaving less time and energy for other priorities. The arrival of adversity, therefore, validates the depth and transformative potential of your magic. You've caused a change and now the system needs to recalibrate. While manifestation tends to follow the path of least resistance, transformation surfaces that within us that blocks our intention. We cannot escape or elude this, but we can explore it, understand its nature, and make it into our companion and ally. When you cast spells and change the balance in life, prepare to observe what comes up in response so you can better adapt yourself to a workable balance.

Resistance to Change

So it is that resistance is inevitable with big changes. For example, if we've come to realize that drinking alcohol is a huge problem in life and decide to make a drastic change in consumption, we're going to have resistance. It could look like inner resistance, anxious parts worried about how to manage life without alcohol: How will I relax? Will my friends like me? How will I deal with all the feelings that alcohol numbed? Those parts may create tension, cravings, depression, and other kinds of pushing back against the change. This could look like outer resistance, where people may keep offering drinks or dismissing our concerns: "It's not a big deal. One drink won't hurt you." They might get weird and uncomfortable around us when they're drinking or react as though we're judging them for drinking. "Get off your high horse and have a beer."

Remember the mobile. Changing a behavior destabilizes everything within you that depended upon that consistency. Drinking might have been a flawed solution to an entirely different problem, and now you'll have to look at the imbalances of that problem and find a new way to create harmony. This change might surprise others in your life who see no reason to change but feel uncomfortable with you not joining them in the familiar rituals. You decided to change, and they did not, but now they must go through their own process in adapting to this new balance. They might try to get you to give up and go back to how things were, which happens a lot and is not necessarily conscious or malicious. (We have this natural tendency to want to maintain homeostasis, even if it's killing us, because change requires energy and effort.) Should you engage your will to sustain your changes, your inner and outer system will adjust. Your health and improved mood might make cravings easier to ignore. The grieving of old comforts may give way to new self-love. Your friends may learn to enjoy time without drinking. Your friends might never be able to accept you, so you find better friends.

So it is that casting a spell confronts us with seeming obstacles to its manifestation. Sustaining your resolve in the face of these challenges is daunting. Here's a fairy tale showing one way forward through resistance and adversity:

The Girl Who Got Away

There once was a little girl who lived in a witch's cabin. This was not a cool, fun witch; rather, she was one who long ago became too embittered by life to treat others as though they were people. For as long as the girl knew, she had always been with the witch—always cleaning, scrubbing, sleeping on hay, and eating what scraps the witch deigned to give her after meals. Walls encircled the witch's cabin, with a rusty gate as the sole entrance and exit to the land. For most of the girl's days, her view was this dull, gray, stony wall. But one day, she'd grown tall enough that she could see over the top, and she was stunned. In the distance she saw a brilliant blue sky. Mountains. The sun, which had always been a dull orb overhead, flamed with bright colors as it rose. Exquisite feelings entranced the girl for which she did not have the words, but I can tell you they were longing and desire.

In the following days, the girl thought often of the blue sky, the sharp mountains. She desperately wanted to see them closer but knew the witch would never let her go. Once a month, the witch left the girl behind while she went to town to trade and get necessities. Whenever the girl wanted to go with her, the witch would slap her across the face and tell her all the chores she should do instead with her time. For so long, this had been life. Now the girl realized she was imprisoned.

One day, while the witch took her afternoon nap, the girl snuck out the door and tried to steal through the gate. But the gate squealed loudly. "Oh, my hinges are so rusty! Oil me! Oil me!" Within seconds, the witch's strong hand was upon the girl's shoulder and she was dragged back into the cabin.

The girl waited until the witch took her next nap and decided to skip the gate by trying to climb over the wall. But upon the wall lived the witch's cat, bedraggled and entangled with burrs, who saw the girl and yowled, "I'm a mess! Please comb my fur!" Again, the girl felt the witch's strong hand dragging her back.

So the girl waited for several days until the witch slept and the cat had gone on its daily hunt so she could slip over the wall and run toward that blue sky. But before she could imagine she was safe, she found herself snarled in the branches of an old apple true, who groaned, "Please lighten my load! I am so heavy with fruit, and my branches are so twisted and tangled." Again, the tree's groaning was enough to wake the witch, who dragged the girl back.

The girl despaired. Every time, she was closer and closer to her desire, and the disappointment of being pulled back was bitter in her heart. But she could not forget the feeling in her heart when she saw the sky. So she waited until the witch left for her monthly trip to town. The girl grabbed a basket and in it she put oil and a rag, a saucer and a bottle of milk, a comb, and a set of pruning shears. Though the girl knew her time was precious, she stopped at the gate and used the oil and rag to clean and grease the rusty hinges until it opened quietly and easily. "Thank you, little one," sighed the gate.

Past the gate, the girl put down the saucer and filled it with milk, calling the cat to her. Gently, carefully, the girl combed the burrs from the cat's coat until it was glossy and smooth. "Thank you, little one," purred the cat.

Then, arriving at the apple tree, the girl took the pruning shears and thinned the snarled branches so that there was room to grow and taste the sun. She plucked the heaviest, ripest apples from the tree's branches to fill her now-empty basket. The tree shivered with pleasure. "Thank you, little one," whispered the tree.

But no sooner had she finished this last task than the girl heard the witch's shrieking cries from the cabin. The witch had arrived home from town and was enraged to find the girl had escaped once again. So the witch turned to run, but found the gate closed and unwilling to budge.

"Open up! Let me out!" shouted the witch. "I need to catch my little serving girl, that ungrateful wretch!"

"I don't know who you mean," said the gate. "But I cannot open now. There are wolves outside."

Cursing, the witch crawled over the wall. Her hair was plaited and bound with a black ribbon that caught on the wall and pulled loose, but she did not have time to worry. Upon landing on the ground, the witch called for her cat.

"Where did the girl go?"

The cat shrugged and sleepily licked its gorgeous fur. "I don't know who you mean."

"I need to catch my little serving girl, that ungrateful wretch!" In frustration, the witch reached out to try to shake the cat, but the cat hissed and bit at her, swiping at the witch's braid and loosening her hair into a wild tail that whipped behind her as she ran. But suddenly the witch felt stopped, unable to run further. Her hair was entangled with the branches of the apple tree and she was caught like a fly in a spider's web.

"Let me go!" shouted the witch. "I need to catch my little serving girl, that ungrateful wretch!"

"I don't know who you mean," said the tree. "But there are pruning shears beside you. You can cut yourself free."

Except the witch could not quite reach the shears, and it took several long minutes to get them in hand and cut her hair free from its knot. By then, the girl had run far beyond the witch's ability to track her. She found the blueness of the sky, the beauty of the mountains, and more besides.

EXERCISE
Reflection

After reading this story, journal about the following questions: Has there ever been a time in life where you felt like the little girl, captive to what prevented you from knowing your desire? When you've tried to escape that captivity, what has snatched you back? What oppositions made it harder to escape? In what ways did or might you have befriended them and made them your allies?

Unexpected Consequences

Because we cannot change one thing without it affecting everything else, we cannot fully understand what will happen as a result of our magic. We don't know what changes our changes will cause. As an example: One of the most successful workings I've done for another person was a case study in unexpected consequences. I had a boyfriend who wanted to sell his condo for an ambitious price. I offered him a whole candle spell to do, and he managed to get exactly his asking price, though he'd almost lowered the price out of fear. Within a month of the working and sale, our relationship ended in drama and turmoil. In the aftermath, while processing our heartbreak and whether to try again, my ex wondered if the spell had caused the breakup. He was coming from a more superstitious place, but I considered it. The intention had been toward eliminating obstacles to his wealth, and our relationship may have been one such obstacle. We'd been looking for houses together, itself a fraught process exposing problems in the relationship. The spell did not create those problems; rather, the spell made it impossible to keep ignoring them.

Seeing these experiences as a "lesson" implies there's a divine teacher out there testing you and putting you through grueling ordeals until you learn a specific truth that's being concealed from you until you figure it out yourself. That sucks. That's a sign of a bad teacher. Instead, I would say that when we come to these situations with curiosity and a willingness to learn, we grow. There is much to learn from any experience for those who are receptive. What you're learning is what's useful for you in your growth and continued practice. You might learn how to set a boundary, how to compromise, how to forgive, or how to confront a person and insist on an apology. You might learn how to accept failure gracefully, or how to keep persisting in spite of setbacks. Life isn't a series of pop quizzes. It's a choose-your-own adventure.

The Law of Maximum Inconvenience

There is one law governing the timing of certain desired and needed events that I have not yet seen written down. It could be summarized thus: *That which you need to occur will do so in a time and manner that is most inconvenient for you.* This law particularly governs contingencies. Imagine flirting with an exciting person and finally making your move on a Monday, texting, "I'm free this weekend. Do you want to hang out?" By Wednesday you have not received a response and your friends ask if you will hang out Saturday night. You don't want to spend the weekend alone, but you still hope this nonresponsive hottie will be free. How long do you wait to make plans? Finally, on Friday morning, you message your friends and commit. "Let's do it. Meet at my place Saturday at five for happy hour, then we'll go out." According to the Law of Maximum Inconvenience, within the next hour your prospective lover will message you something like, "Sorry I missed this! I'd love to see you! I'm busy tonight but let's get dinner Saturday night!"

This law falls under the purview of trickster god and planet Mercury, governing contingencies around timely communications and transportation: waiting for messages, waiting for the bus, waiting for a job opportunity. Back when I was a smoker and rode public buses, I could be certain that the bus would arrive within seconds of lighting my cigarette, but it would be delayed if I held off. Insofar as this law is real, one lesson I take from it is that the tension and waiting for what is sought becomes an obstacle to its appearance. The energy of wanting things too much, being too attached and growing increasingly more annoyed or desperate becomes a blockage. As soon as we give up, all that tension drains away and suddenly the spigot turns on and life flows again. I admit this perspective is suspiciously evocative of an attitude that I critique elsewhere in the book—that your particular impatience-warped reality makes the bus late and affects you and everyone else depending upon it for commuting. ("Thanks a lot! You should've lit your cigarette minutes ago!")

Yet perhaps this law returns us to meditate upon the twins of destiny and fate. It invites us to stop being so rigid and accept the flow—the only magic that neutralizes this law—and embrace inconvenience, focusing on what we can control, and flowing with change. So much stress comes from wanting everything to be just so and imagining that a magical life will make our personal schedule frictionless. It's a beautiful moment when you go ahead and make plans with your friends on Saturday and it turns out your love interest is free on Friday, so you have a perfect weekend. Yet it could be totally okay for other things to happen, or even better. Your friends might be excited about the date and happy for you to cancel your plans with them. Your prospective love might be totally understanding about the schedule conflict and willing to find a time that works for both of you. Or they respond poorly, and you learn they aren't good for you. The deepest lesson of the Law of Maximum Inconvenience is to accept that life is messy and to avoid putting life and needs on pause while waiting for what can't be controlled.

Assessing Magical Results

Believing that magic always works helps me explore when spells look like failures. Unfortunately, failure does not always give useful feedback. At times, all we learn is that what we tried didn't work. It's rare and a gift when there is clear feedback about what didn't work and how we could do it better next time. Instead, we must keep throwing things into the aether and see what gets results. Instead of getting hung up on stories about my incompetence, however, I could see the failure as data. Trying and failing gives you more information than you had when you hadn't made any attempt. We can look back with a cool, witchy eye and see what comes to our attention. What if your current experience is exactly what your particular working manifested? What if your expectations of what it would look like were wrong? What if the prevailing currents of fate were too hostile to your working, resulting in a weaker expression? What could you learn about intention, process, and the conditions of your working?

It's normal to have hard feelings when you don't get what you want or get things you absolutely didn't want. You may have hard feelings even when you get what you want. One year I thought

I wanted to go to graduate school to get an MFA in creative writing, and I did gestation magic that included the desire for financial stability. Notably, I did not specifically name that I wanted to be getting a graduate degree. During that year, I absolutely was not able to get into any of the programs I wanted (in retrospect, this was a blessing). But when I opened my envelope, I realized I was financially stable, with a decent income and savings—which I absolutely would not have had if I had started graduate school.

EXERCISE
Contemplating the Results of a Spell

Whether your manifestations are abundant or mild, use the following questions for contemplation on a piece of spell-work: How did your intention relate to the prevailing currents of fate? Did historical, economic, spiritual, or social realities impede the path of your manifestation? (Example: Trying to start a new career in the midst of a recession.) Could there have been a major conflict between the desires you seeded? (Example: My desire for financial stability and my desire to take on loads of debt for a graduate degree that wouldn't have helped my earning potential.) Could a different process of spellwork have remedied these impediments? (This is up for interpretation and there may not be a right answer, but I find it an interesting question for divination and reflection.)

Finally, consider: What conditions in your life got in the way of this manifestation? Are you willing or able to change even one of these conditions? What do you fear might happen if you made these changes? Is it better to work to accept your life as it is?

Discernment with the Triple Soul

When facing any kind of adversity or confusion in your workings, it's good to take a pause and work through a discernment practice. We might have a messy ball of yarn that appears knotted and stuck, and though the desire is to throw it away or cut through it, there's great power in taking the time to detangle the threads, lay them beside each other, and see what you've got. Stepping back to detangle and assess each thread offers the clarity we need to move forward. There are multiple ways to practice discernment.[34] Whereas divination is about asking for information and guidance from an external source, discernment is more about looking at what you know from a different perspective to gain more understanding. There is a connotation of sifting through—like detangling yarn—in which the process of discerning separates out the elements of the situation so that you can see with clarity what is before you.

As we have spoken much about the triple soul in this book, let's take this opportunity to connect with those parts of us—animal, human, and divine—to separate out the lenses through which they view adversity. Looking through each lens separately offers a depth of perspective that we do not get when they're enmeshed. Through the animal soul we perceive energetic, emotional, and instinctive truths inherent in the problem. Through the human soul we perceive logical, ideological, cultural, and communal qualities of the problem. Through the god soul we perceive spiritual qualities of the problem, as well as the perspective of our older, wiser part of self.

---

34. I write more of other perspectives on discernment practice in my book *Circling the Star*, 108–111.

Perceiving Through Three Lenses

As always, find a place where you can be safe and relatively uninterrupted for twenty minutes or so. Consider a problem that is appearing for you in any domain of life, whether it is an everyday struggle or a magical or spiritual dilemma.

Part One

Slow your breathing down. With every exhale, let your body relax into the ground upon which you sit or stand. Sense or imagine that there is energy surrounding and interpenetrating your body, extending a few centimeters out from your skin. Contemplate this energetic body, your double, in which your animalistic, instinctive, and child energies find their home. Breathe energy into your core, between your navel and pelvis, and breathe it out into the body surrounding your body. Sense the edges of this instinctive soul. Imagine it has its own eyes, ears, and mouth extending from yours. Ask this part of your soul to reveal itself to you—to show you its condition, its qualities, its elemental world. Ask it what it does for you. Ask what you can do for it to support and strengthen it. Thank this soul.

With your breath, let your awareness move outward to a part of your soul extending several more centimeters in every direction, forming a sphere or an egg-shape around your body. Contemplate this part of your soul, in which your rational, intellectual, and communal energies find expression. This part communicates information out into the world and receives information for you. Breathe energy into your heart and out to cleanse this part of your soul, touching its edges. Ask this part of your soul to reveal itself to you—to show you its condition, its qualities, its elemental world. Ask it what it does for you. Ask what you can do for it to support and strengthen it. Thank this soul.

With your breath, let your awareness rise up to a spot slightly above your head. Imagine a sphere floating above, making contact with your head and other soul parts. Contemplate this part of your soul, in which your divine nature rests. Here is the god soul carrying the wisdom of your ancestors and your previous lifetimes, and your connection to God Herself. Breathe energy into your head and out to open your crown to better allow connection with this part of your soul. Ask this part of your soul to reveal itself to you—to show you its condition, its qualities, its elemental world. Ask it what it does for you. Ask what you can do for it to support and strengthen it. Thank this soul.

Part Two

Breathing deeply, let your awareness return to the center in your core, near your pelvis. Think of the problem you would like to explore and imagine that problem sitting in your belly. Notice how that feels in your animal soul that surrounds your body. Ask it what it wants you to know about this problem. When you feel you've received an answer, imagine the problem rising from your belly into the center of your chest. Notice how it feels in the rational soul that extends outward in that spherical shape. Notice if the way the problem appears to you is different in any way. Notice how your rational soul responds to the problem. Ask it what it wants you to know about this problem. When things feel complete, imagine the problem rising from your heart into the center of your head. Notice how it feels to the god soul floating above you. Notice, again, if the problem changes its form or appearance in this center. Notice how your god soul responds to the problem. Ask what it wants you to know about this problem. Thank your souls.

Imagine you can set this problem entirely outside of your body now, in front of you. Send a breath up to your god soul and feel the breath returning, bringing all of your souls into alignment with each other. Imagine looking through the eyes of your animal soul, connected to your divinity and protected by your humanity. Notice how the problem changes when you perceive it from this view. Notice how you change in relationship to the problem. Let this go and bring yourself back to grounded awareness. Feel the earth under you. Drink water. Journal about what you experienced and what you've learned in this process. What does this information tell you about your relationship with the problem? What needs to be done?

Chapter 13

RELEASING AND RENEWING

I'm a person who loves a clean surface and a messy junk drawer where all my uncategorized objects live. Clutter is difficult for me. After making magic my life, however, my shelves and altars began to accumulate odds and ends. Statues, art, bottles of sprays, oils, and potions, trinkets and stones, the occasional bundle tied with a string of colored yarn gathered in corners. Amulets and talismans pile up, their purpose distantly remembered. All of these carry memories, intentions, and life force from so many moments of personal work or community empowerment. There is merit in taking time to sort through these pieces of magic and assess whether they still serve. Certain pieces of magic may stay alive for decades, while others serve their purpose and dissipate. As the butterfly discards the cocoon, so too may we release the materials that housed our transformations. The you who you are today was within the you who did that magic, in seed form, and that magic was necessary to let you sprout, flower, and fruit. So honor it, but allow yourself to ask if it still serves you today. When we do slow magic, we periodically need to review the magic that once sustained us. In this chapter, we will be using the same processes for evaluating old dreams, goals, and spells. All of these spur us into transformation and bind us to action, and all require reflection and revision from time to time.

EXERCISE

Reassessing Your Magic

Look at a piece of magic that has been with you for a long time: an old spell that has been on your altar; a desire that has been persistently with you but often falls off the priority list; an old dream that you've been following for years; a long-term working that persists; even a goal that you castigate yourself for not pursuing. Hold a related physical object if you have one. Otherwise imagine you can gather the energy of it into your hands or heart and be in relationship with it. Let it remind you of its intent and history in your life. Ask yourself, "Does this serve me in my life today?"

Notice what comes up for you. Try to name the ways it does serve you and the ways it does not. If it's helpful, set the object before you and make notes. Breathe into your center and feel how the energy of this spell, dream, or goal affects your body. Notice how it feels to imagine recommitting, and how it feels to imagine letting this go. Give yourself permission for it to become a choice. If you notice that neither recommitment nor release feels right, ask yourself what needs to change to make this work for you again. After this assessment stage, you may choose to renew your commitment to the work, renegotiate the conditions of the work, or release the work entirely.

Renewing

When I was seven years old, I found solace in books and started to explore creating my own stories. It was around that time I decided that I wanted to be a writer. This was my first dream in life and one made with all the measured thoughtfulness and consideration that a child tends to muster. Unlike other perfectly good dreams I had (being a fireman or a plumber), the desire to be a writer stuck with me and became an identity that I wore. Others saw that I had an affinity with words and supported my goal to be a writer, which was a wonderful gift. I spent much of my time in my head, narrating life as it happened, imagining how I would put my experiences into language. This was years before the internet was accessible to the public, or else I might have been publicly oversharing my life much sooner. I pursued writing as my undergraduate major in college and thought I'd continue into making it my life. Except now I was starting to get a sense of adult responsibilities and met real writers to get a glimpse of their lives, their characters, and the sacrifices they made to be authors. Something in me balked. Writing alone is not sustainable for life unless you are great at marketing and self-promotion or you happen to be lucky and strike it big, especially if you get a movie or television deal, something most writers do not achieve.

What's more, I went through a phase of hating writing. It felt stressful and obligatory. When I failed to get into graduate school to continue studying writing, I stepped back and looked at my relationship to the work. Having gone through a more literature-focused program, my writing had become oriented toward impressing and reflecting what was popular in literary circles. No longer was it an expression of myself or a source of joy. I decided to abandon writing as a primary career and find other work that would give me enough money to do the kind of writing that gave me pleasure. Since then, there have been numerous times when I struggled to prioritize writing and resented the pressure I felt to keep doing it. Yet I found that when I did write, it settled me into myself. It was much like my meditation and exercise practices—a little effort could offer more clarity, space, and vitality. But I have to allow it to remain an honest choice, not a draining obligation. When magic, goals, or dreams feel like draining chores and obligations, they're no longer feeding us, and it does not necessarily mean we've outgrown them. At times it's about remembering there is choice, and we can reconnect and recommit to what we love.

EXERCISE
Renewing Your Magic

This ritual is for when you have a spell, dream, or goal that still feels alive and you decide to recommit. Again, if you have a physical object connected to this working, place it before you. Otherwise imagine the form of this dream, goal, or spell before you; or you could picture the part of you that carries this working. Gather the energy of the working within you and breathe it into the object or image. Take three breaths, first enlivening and expanding your belly, then your heart, then your head. Take another breath, sending cords of connection from these three centers to the energy of this working. Say, "I honor you. I welcome you. I choose you." Find an achievable way you can continue honoring this working and promise yourself you will do it. Let the energy of the working return to your body and dissolve into you, or let it be absorbed into the object that holds this intention for you.

Renegotiating

I've had dreams of my future self that now feel embarrassing to admit. When I was younger and on fire with reading about civil rights activists, I fantasized that one day I'd be one of those fierce frontline leaders. Yet it was always "one day," a dream that aroused as much terror as it did excitement. What I tended to do in practice was either be another body in the protest or do more behind the scenes work. During the civil unrest of early COVID, there was a great deal of activism happening in my city, and I felt like I was supposed to be involved. However, I didn't have trusted allies who could march with me and support me if things went awry. I reached out to friends who either had their own buddies or otherwise could not participate. It occurred to me that I tend to act on things that are important to me. I invest my energy and discipline in it. I am stubborn as hell. So I had to admit that my disconnection from the activist community showed me that I was not called to direct protesting work. Those savior fantasies did not accomplish anything tangible. Yet the work of forming a world of love and connection without coercion enlivens me. I needed to reexamine my assumptions of what activism was supposed to look like and what I had to offer as well as renegotiate that goal to be one more congruent with who I am.

EXERCISE
Renegotiating Your Magic

This ritual is for when you have a spell, dream, or goal that you need to renegotiate to one more aligned with this moment in your life. Look again at your list of the ways this work serves you and does not serve you. What conditions need to change to address the ways it doesn't serve and enhance the ways it does? For a moment, set aside all the questions of practicality and imagine: if you could do whatever you wanted with no consequences, how would you engage with this work? You might want to journal, voice dictate, or process with a trusted colleague.

When you have a sense of what feels workable, talk to the work. Place the associated physical object before you, or imagine the form of this dream, goal, or spell, or imagine the part of you that carries this working. Gather the energy of the work within you and breathe it into the object or image. Tell the work what you'd need to be different and how you want to honor this work in your life today. Ask what it needs from you to support this change, and listen to judge whether you are able to honor the request. Keep in mind that we're doing magic here, so if the request is physically impossible, know that you can honor it in the imaginal realms where the limits are far fewer.

Take three breaths, first enlivening and expanding your belly, then your heart, then your head. Take another breath, sending cords of connection from these three centers to the energy of this working. Say, "Thank you for being with me in this life." Formalize the new agreement by stating your new desire and promise to honor the work. Let the energy of the working return to your body and dissolve into you, or let it be absorbed into the object that holds this intention for you.

Releasing

Once a spell has gone through its full flowering and fruition, we have the seeds for future work and the materials that nurtured and made those seeds possible. That material can continue to feed and nurture the new seeds of magic, but not if we're holding on to the old forms and doing nothing with them. We need energetic house-keeping. Keeping old spells is like keeping pictures of ex-partners on the refrigerator door while dating new people. There are times when they're simply sweet mementos of people who matter. And there also times, let's be honest, when those photos are a reminder of unfinished business that keeps alive a vague sense of guilt or longing for what you once had. If the latter is the case, it's going to be difficult to welcome new connections into your life until you've done more work grieving and releasing the old. Discharging and releasing old magic allows it to dissolve and return to your vitality, or to the body of the earth, or to the being of God Herself, where it becomes the soil for new forms and possibilities.

EXERCISE

Releasing Your Magic

This ritual can serve to discharge and release old spells, dreams, and goals. My process is gratitude, release or reabsorption, and then disposal. Gratitude is simple. Take in hand the object associated with your magic—or, again, imagine the form of your dream, goal, or spell before you. Say thank you. Appreciate the way it has served you. This spell, dream, or goal has been alive and inspirited, and now you will be giving it death. Give it a nice send-off. Then hold the object or image and imagine its energy draining back into your body. For certain works this will not feel right, especially ones related to cursing. In that case, you have options. I have a green cube associated with the element of earth into which I put old spells to release their energy and compost. Or I release the energies into the air and ask God Herself to reabsorb them. Or I ask Anubis to take it. Dogs will eat anything.

Dispose of the material remains in a way that feels honorable and safe. Some witches consider throwing it in the garbage to be improper, and I agree it can be a rude send-off. If that's the best option available, and you've followed this process, by now all that's left anyway is waste. Don't stress about it. Reusable materials might be bathed in salt and moonlight to be purified of their old intentions and left fresh for new use—rocks and crystals in particular. If you can recycle or compost, that better supports the intention of recirculating old energy to become new matter. So too is burning, burying, or releasing in water to be dissolved. Make sure the material will not harm the environment where you leave it. You could also leave the material at a crossroads. Be mindful that someone will have to physically dispose of it if it does not decompose on its own. Try not to screw them over.

Awakening

Releasing old motivations brings up grief. Our younger selves may feel betrayed when we give up what they wanted so badly. Old vows to never be like those people who give up must now be altered. Old urges to be special, pay a debt, prove ourselves, earn approval, or cling to love may no longer motivate our adult selves. In these instances, I ask the question: if my younger self got what he wanted, what would that make possible? If I lived in a world where I was special or my debts were paid or I was loved and valued by those who had withheld it before—what would I do then? Life is not guaranteed, and we do not have enough time and energy to explore every possibility. That is a sorrow, and a freedom. God soul gathers up these unrealized dreams to make them into new magic—new dreams, or very old dreams that we'd set aside.

The releasing of the old thus makes possible what before seemed unimaginable: opportunities for play, experimentation, or living that were not previously accessible. We may find we have the money, time, and energy to live these dreams. Let's not let ideas about age get in the way of being alive. I never liked sports or ath-leticism because I was so bad at them. But after years of working to build a stable career, I took up martial arts in my late thirties as a way of dealing with my feelings about the political turmoil in my country. My movements were awkward, stiff, and easily startled by fast, aggressive attacks. I didn't believe I would get far, but my goal in those first few months was to attend at least once a week for an entire class. I marveled at the people who could fly through the air, skim across the ground, and get back up for more without injury or upset. I wondered what it would be like to do that and made that my next goal. I continued like that—next goal after next goal—until one day I preparing to test for black belt.

Now in my forties, it seems clearer that the less I care about what happens, the more I tend to get what I want. It seems harsh and strange, but true. Younger me resented being told such things. I would feel blamed for being anxious or afraid, and then I'd feel even more tense and worried I'd never be able to relax and get what I need. What an unfortunate trap. My aikido journey to black belt became another opportunity to learn this secret. For the year or so prior to my test, I ran the gamut of feelings. Some of my peers started later than me and moved faster through the ranks. This brought out my competitive urges and all that old shame about not being athletic. Whenever I made mistakes, I got frustrated and chided myself, which led to more mistakes. There were days I left the dojo believing I did not belong there, and that everyone knew it and were humor-ing me. All those stressed, critical, and attached parts of me felt like they needed to "prove" I was worthy of black belt.

In the month before I decided I would test, I sat down to think about what I wanted. The desire I named was to be celebrated by community and recognized for my attainment. I created and charged a sigil for this and allowed myself not to set a specific date of manifestation—it would happen when the time was right. A few days later, fate intervened when I got COVID. It was a relatively mild case, but it compelled me to isolate at home and do nothing but rest for a week. Sitting in my ill body, I could see with new clarity. I'd been taking it all too seriously. No one needed me to "prove" I was worthy of a black belt. Whether I tested this month or later, I would pass if I kept trying. My health recovered fairly quickly, thankfully, and when I did test, I went in open to any outcome but with pride in myself that I was trying something difficult.

I passed. I had a great test, flowing and powerful and unencumbered by all that stress and self-doubt. Sensei said wonderful things about my performance and my community applauded for me. I stood in the full flowering of my spell after I had stopped needing it to come true. This experience taught me, yet again, to take it slow, to engage will while moving with the unexpected twists of fate. This achievement reaches back through several cycles of magic to that first intention that opened this book, when I wanted to "be hot." If I hadn't begun on that seemingly superficial path, I wouldn't have learned to enjoy moving my body. The path of desire is a fire that constantly renews itself upon what once fed it. What I hope this story illustrates is the breadth of desires worthy of slow magic. Today, there is so much noise around manifestation coaches and wealth that it seems easy to forget that money isn't the only goal. There is nothing wrong with doing magic for money, but what would that money make possible in your life? There's a seed worth a spell.

CONCLUSION

This book emerged from almost two decades of magic and set-backs. I would not say that my life has been without privilege and unearned favor, but I would also say that adversity has always been on the path beside me. Growing up in a time of relative peace and affluence to emerge into an adulthood of economic and political upheaval has been a bracing experience. There were times when I struggled to believe in myself at all, and I was fortunate to have the belief of others to push me forward. With this background, I have always had complicated feelings whenever I talk to another spiritual "manifestation" type who espouses some variation of the belief that whenever you are truly on your path and aligned with purpose, manifestation is easy, natural, and joyful. This has rarely been the case, in my experience. More common has been the feeling that in doing magic, I must both work *and* pay for results.

In the contrast between ease and work in magic I see an opposition of—can you guess?—the divine twins, and here I would characterize them as Jupiter and Saturn. Jupiterian magic has that beautiful flow of luck and alignment and a sense of higher purpose. Saturnian magic has friction, adversities, and consequences, and demands commitment and steadiness. Saturn looms large in my chart, scowling at all those other planets that dare to try to actualize their desires without a good measure of adversity and discipline. In writing this book, I want to encourage those like me not to let setbacks and struggles make us feel like we're not magical enough, don't know our purpose, or don't deserve the things we want. But I have also lived long enough to see my beautiful jovian friends unwittingly thrust into saturnian circumstances, and I want them to know, too, there is a path forward. It was coming out of the apocalyptic upheaval of the years leading up to and following the outbreak of COVID-19 that opened the seed of this book for it to sprout into my conscious mind and come to flower in these words. Social and political norms that seemed stable and taken for granted as resolved were suddenly upended. Ideologies and positions once considered fringe now showed up in the news, in the mouths of elected officials, in law. The cycle of history turns again, and currents we thought weak and terminating have erupted with fresh force. Yet this will not be the end. The spiral continues to turn. Times of constriction and loss show us what gains have stabilized in the long arc and reveal opportunities for transformation and growth that will prepare us for the next turning.

Practicing aikido continues to challenge me into this resolution of will and endurance. My teachers frequently challenged the lack of energy and vigor I'd put into my attacks and the ways my body would disconnect and collapse too quickly. The practice is to commit fully to the attack and to stay connected and aware during the entire technique. If I'm being pressed down but my partner relaxes their grip, I rise up as much as I'm allowed. This movement increases my own safety, makes their technique more dramatic and effective, and keeps open the possibility for escape and reversal. Even in moments when I am almost completely pinned and immobilized, there might be a hole in their technique that lets me completely change the relationship. So if you know your intention and desire and practice with vigor, there is never a giving up so much as patiently staying engaged until you see your opportunity. This is also slow magic.

There are two important connotations to slow magic throughout this work. One is of magic that is enduring, long lasting, and executed over time. The other is of magic that slows us down. It may feel like another paradox to move slowly for results that you expect to come slowly. So much of our culture in this moment emphasizes speed, efficiency, and declaring everything to be a crisis that needs immediate rectification. Living in this way is being caught in a tangle of knots and trying to get free with wild pulling. It only makes us more stuck. This book invites us to cultivate patience, deliberation, presence, and long-term vision, to turn toward this tangle of knots and while breathing, slowly work our way free. In this way, moving slowly may end up being the quicker path.

In this book, we have looked at maps of the inner and outer worlds to get clarity about desire and orient ourselves in magic and will. Working with our souls and our parts, repairing ancestral lineages, befriending spirits who can help us understand what is hard to perceive—all of these help us grasp magic and desire. We invite curiosity at every stage, about what our experiences teach us about who we are and what we want. We practice presence when receiving our desires, taking in the nourishment of the fruits of our efforts and discerning the seeds of our next move. We've also explored mapping the world without, particularly the larger contradictions of life and magic. Attending to these contradictions without trying to solve them makes us more flexible and expansive. We have a role to play in life, and our efforts are necessary. There is simultaneously much beyond our power to manage, and we are one cell in the great body of God Herself. So when the currents of magic do not flow in alignment with will, we can take ease and gauge where the river will take us.

Magic is at its heart a volitional act, an act of agency in the world in which we make things happen on purpose. That is the foundation of will. Yet as we pursue will, we experience the contradictions of a world in which we are powerful and powerless, embodied in the twins of destiny and fate. Accepting the powers and limits of both allows us to evolve in relationship with our conditions. We have looked at tools of divination, intention setting, and bold action in following this transformative path of desire. We have looked at how linear time offers a trajectory that looks like fate until we break up the root systems and open up visions for a different future. We have looked at the cycles upon cycles that govern magic, life, and history, so that we can align ourselves with the prevailing winds of our season to propel magic forward. We have looked at the spiral that lifts us from smallness into increasing power, possibility, and perspective. As we deepen our practice, we have expanded our awareness of being and doing as companions in life. Allowing both to serve us, rather than fight each other, establishes the rhythms that let our energy flow. We have explored the human and other-than-human relationships that join our personal wills to the greater wills that carry our magic forward. We have practiced assessing our magic to find where it is in our cycles and find areas we could grow in strength and wisdom. We reflected on traps and adversities that befall those who walk the path of will, along with ways to get free.

With the tools and teachings offered in this book, you can go forward in the work of creating a life that honors your dignity and divine worth. You could work toward the manifestation of a loving, prosperous family. You could enchant into being a trade school program that earns you a good wage and a stable career. You could gather a cadre of dedicants to your beloved god and anchor their presence in your community. You could unbind the wounds of your ancestors and their limits on your power, self-esteem, and potential. You could find your own will, one far more interesting and exciting than I can imagine for you, and follow its path. I deeply want all of us to win, to be happy, to engender healthy and hardy descendants, strong and supportive communities, loving families, moving works of art, and fascinating technologies. I believe that if we were truly being ourselves and expressing our divine purpose, there would be room for everyone. We would recognize that we have all we need and have much to offer each other. We would not need to bind ourselves to another's desires. We would not need to coerce others into serving our dreams. Our dreams would be expansive enough to have room for everyone else's. We could work together, knowing we belong, knowing that our individual wills braid together into the strongest rope. We could manifest liberation from poverty and from dependence on technologies that threaten the lives of our descendants and our kin in the plant and animal realms.

What future would your desire create? When I am living into the future of my desire, I see a world in which so many of us do important work caring for each other, repairing the hurts we've caused, creating works of beauty and inspiration, and tending lineages of magic that keep us alive and awake. Through such contemplation, my heart evokes that future into existence by discovering it in this moment. The mystery of slow magic is in dreaming of a world that may never be fully manifested while accepting the reality of the place in which we live. In doing our magic to bridge those two realms, we make this moment and this world beautiful. We dwell in our most integrated, authentic selves, honoring our essence and our place in the larger currents of God Herself. We become a magnet drawing toward us that which that honors our desire. There is a moment when all is exactly as it must be. All the awfulness of the past seems a worthwhile price to pay for this moment. We feel a hope made of steel, earned through our effort and success. And then the moment passes. The peacock divides out into the twins. Struggle returns. We return to our practice.

BIBLIOGRAPHY

Abraham-Hicks. "Abraham on Martin Luther King." March 6, 2008, https://www.youtube.com/watch?v=kBB5UzdO5es.

Achtziger, Anja, Thorsten Fehr, Gabriele Oettingen, Peter M. Gollwitzer, and Brigitte Rockstroh. "Strategies of intention formation are reflected in continuous MEG activity." *Social Neuroscience* 4, no. 1 (2009): 11–27. https://doi.org/10.1080/17470910801925350.

Arnsten, Amy F. T. "Stress signalling pathways that impair prefrontal cortex structure and function." *Nature Reviews Neuroscience* 10, no. 6 (2009): 410–422. https://doi.org/10.1038/nrn2648.

Beckett, John. "The Storm is Strengthening—Put Your Faith in Deeper Things." *Under the Ancient Oaks* (blog), April 24, 2018. https://www.patheos.com/blogs/johnbeckett/2018/04/the-storm-is-strengthening-put-your-faith-in-deeper-things.html.

Betz, Hans Dieter. *The Greek Magical Papyri in Translation.* 2nd ed. University of Chicago Press, 1992.

Cacioppo, John, and William Patrick. *Loneliness: Human Nature and the Need for Social Connection.* W. W. Norton & Company, 2008.

Coyle, T. Thorn. *Evolutionary Witchcraft.* Weiser Books, 2004.

Coyle, T. Thorn. *Kissing the Limitless: Deep Magic and the Great Work of Transforming Yourself and the World.* Weiser Books, 2009.

———. *Make Magic of Your Life: Passion, Purpose, and the Power of Desire.* Weiser, 2013.

———. *Sigil Magic: For Writers and Other Creatives.* PF Publishing, 2015.

Csikszentmihalyi, Mihaly. *Flow: The Psychology of Optimal Experience.* HarperCollins, 2008.

Dominguez, Jr., Ivo. *Practical Astrology for Witches and Pagans.* Red Wheel/Weiser, 2016.

Duriel, Durgadas Allon. *The Little Work: Magic to Transform Your Everyday Life.* Llewellyn Publications, 2020.

Foor, Daniel. *Ancestral Medicine: Rituals for Personal and Family Healing.* Bear & Company, 2017.

Jung, Carl Gustav. *Aion: Researches into the Phenomenology of the Self.* Translated and edited by Gerhard Adler. Routledge, 1981.

King, Jr., Martin Luther. "The Negro Is Your Brother." *The Atlantic Monthly* 212, no. 2 (August 1963): 78–88.

Klein, Howard J., Robert B. Lount, Hee Man Park, and Bryce J. Linford. "When goals are known: The effects of audience relative status on goal commitment and performance." *Journal of Applied Psychology* 105, no. 4 (2020): 372–389.

Koenig-Robert, Roger, and Joel Pearson. "Decoding the contents and strength of imagery before volitional engagement." *Scientific Reports* 9 (2019): 3504.

Preuss, Todd, and Steven Wise. "Evolution of prefrontal cortex." *Neuropsychopharmacology* 47: 3–19. Springer Nature, 2022.

Rella, Anthony. *Circling the Star.* Gods & Radicals, 2018.

Rudhyar, Dane, and Leyla Rael. *Astrological Aspects: A Process-Oriented Approach*. Red Wheel/Weiser, 1980.

Schwartz, Richard. *No Bad Parts*. Sounds True, 2021.

Starhawk. "The Charge of the Goddess." *The Spiral Dance: A Rebirth of the Ancient Religion of the Great Goddess*. HarperCollins, 1999.

Tarnas, Richard. *Cosmos and Psyche: Intimations of a New World View*. Plume, 2006.

Tzu, Lao. *Tao Te Ching*. Translated by Ursula K. Le Guin. Shambhala, 1997.

Valiente, Doreen. "The Charge of the Goddess." *The Charge of the Goddess—The Poetry of Doreen Valiente*. The Doreen Valiente Foundation, 2014.

Welwood, John. "On Spiritual Bypassing and Relationship." Science and Nonduality website. https://www.scienceandnonduality .com/article/on-spiritual-bypassing-and-relationship.

Zakroff, Laura Tempest. *Sigil Witchery: A Witch's Guide to Making Magic Symbols*. Llewellyn Publications, 2018.

Index

To Write to the Author

If you wish to contact the author or would like more information about this book, please write to the author in care of Llewellyn Worldwide Ltd. and we will forward your request. Both the author and publisher appreciate hearing from you and learning of your enjoyment of this book and how it has helped you. Llewellyn Worldwide Ltd. cannot guarantee that every letter written to the author can be answered, but all will be forwarded. Please write to:

Anthony Rella
℅ Llewellyn Worldwide
2143 Wooddale Drive
Woodbury, MN 55125-2989

Please enclose a self-addressed stamped envelope for reply,
or $1.00 to cover costs. If outside the U.S.A., enclose
an international postal reply coupon.

Many of Llewellyn's authors have websites with additional information and resources. For more information, please visit our website at http://www.llewellyn.com